The PARABLES of Jesus

VOLUME 2

CLARENCE SEXTON

CROWN
CHRISTIAN
PUBLICATIONS
Royal Reading

The PARABLES of Jesus

VOLUME 2

FIRST EDITION
COPYRIGHT
AUGUST 2003

CROWN
CHRISTIAN
PUBLICATIONS
Royal Reading

SUNDAY SCHOOL SERIES

THE PARABLES OF JESUS
VOLUME 2
Copyright © 2003
Crown Christian Publications
Powell, Tennessee 37849
ISBN: 1-58981-176-3

Layout and design by Stephen Troell & Joshua Tangeman

All rights reserved. No part of this publication may be reproduced, stored in a retrieval system, or transmitted in any form-electronic, mechanical, photocopy, recording, or any other-except for brief quotations embodied in critical articles or printed reviews, without the prior permission in writing from the publisher.

Printed in the United States of America

God's Word is true. The truth of God's Word must be taught to each generation. This volume is dedicated to my precious grandchildren–Nick, Madison, Alli, Andrew, Justin, and Luke. *"I have no greater joy than to hear that my children walk in truth"* (III John 4).

Chapter One	The Bridegroom	9
Chapter Two	The Sheep and the Goats	19
Chapter Three	The New Cloth on an Old Garment	33
Chapter Four	Who Is Neighbor to Those in Need?	45
Chapter Five	The Rich Fool	55
Chapter Six	Bearing Fruit	67
Chapter Seven	Those Who Are Blessed	83
Chapter Eight	Discipleship	95
Chapter Nine	The Lost Sheep, the Lost Coin, and the Lost Son	107
Chapter Ten	The Lost Son Who Never Left Home	123
Chapter Eleven	The Faithful	137
Chapter Twelve	Mercy	153
Chapter Thirteen	Occupy Till I Come	165

"And at midnight there was a cry made, Behold, the bridegroom cometh; go ye out to meet him."

Matthew 25:6

THE BRIDEGROOM

early one third of the recorded teachings of Jesus Christ are given to us in parables. We must understand the parables of Christ to understand the teaching of Christ. All of His parables are found in the first three Gospel records: the Gospel according to Matthew, the Gospel according to Mark, and the Gospel according to Luke.

Parables are not fables, for parables come from real situations. The word *parable* means "to cast alongside." It is a story cast alongside a spiritual truth to help us understand the spiritual truth. Parables are not allegories. An allegory has some meaning in practically every detail. A parable is not interpreted that way. A parable is a story given with one great truth or great lesson for us. As we study these parables given by the Lord Jesus, we will see that these are the greatest stories ever told.

The Parables of Jesus

The Lord Jesus Christ is coming again. There are three words that will help us to remember important things in the order of our Lord's return. The first word is *appearing.* We speak of His appearing. The second word is *disappearing.* There will be a great disappearing. All those who know the Lord Jesus as their personal Savior will be caught up to be with Him and will disappear from the earth. This is referred to as the Rapture of the Church. The third word is *reappearing.* At the end of the seven-year Tribulation period, we shall reappear. The Bible says in Jude 14-15, *"Behold, the Lord cometh with ten thousands of his saints, to execute judgment upon all, and to convince all that are ungodly among them of all their ungodly deeds which they have ungodly committed."*

The Word of God says in Matthew 25:1-12,

> *Then shall the kingdom of heaven be likened unto ten virgins, which took their lamps, and went forth to meet the bridegroom. And five of them were wise, and five were foolish. They that were foolish took their lamps, and took no oil with them: but the wise took oil in their vessels with their lamps. While the bridegroom tarried, they all slumbered and slept. And at midnight there was a cry made, Behold, the bridegroom cometh; go ye out to meet him. Then all those virgins arose, and trimmed their lamps. And the foolish said unto the wise, Give us of your oil; for our lamps are gone out. But the wise answered, saying, Not so; lest there be not enough for us and you: but go ye rather to them that sell, and buy for yourselves. And while they went to buy, the bridegroom came; and they that were ready went in with him to the marriage: and the door was shut. Afterward came also the other virgins, saying, Lord, Lord, open to us. But he answered and said, Verily I say unto you, I know you not.*

 The Bridegroom

There is some question about whether this parable is dealing with the Rapture, or with the period of time during the Tribulation before the reappearing of Jesus Christ, when every eye shall see Him. The safest position to take is that of Christ coming for His bride, which is referred to as the Rapture.

This is not a parable about service; it is a parable about salvation and about those who will be ready when the Lord returns. Take to heart the message that Jesus Christ gives here and be ready when the Bridegroom comes.

The Bible says in Matthew 25:6, *"And at midnight there was a cry made, Behold, the bridegroom cometh."* In the oriental part of the world, among the Jews

All those who know the Lord Jesus as their personal Savior will be caught up to be with Him and will disappear from the earth.

in particular, the bride was chosen by the groom's father. The couple entered an espousal period as the bride was promised to the groom. During that period of time there was no personal or physical contact between them, and the bridegroom went to prepare a place to live. When the time of preparation was complete, and everything was in order, the bridegroom returned for his bride.

These virgins spoken of in Matthew chapter twenty-five would have been like bridesmaids, waiting for the bridegroom to return for the bride. They would have known something about the time the bridegroom was expected, and they were to wait alertly for him. But in this story, they were all slumbering.

In this oriental or Jewish wedding, we can see the picture of our Lord coming for His bride. Our heavenly Bridegroom is the Lord Jesus Christ. He has a bride chosen by the Father. We have had no contact with our heavenly Bridegroom, as far as physically seeing Him, but we are espoused to Him. He is preparing a mansion for us.

When everything is complete, He will come again and take His bride to be with Him forever. The story of the Jewish wedding is a beautiful picture of what awaits us as the bride of Christ.

THE DIFFERENCE BETWEEN THESE TWO GROUPS

Many call this a complicated parable, but there are some very clear lessons to learn from it. There is one statement given in this parable that declares the difference between these two groups.

We may dwell on the fact that the Bible says that five were wise and five were foolish. We may dwell on the fact that some had oil and others did not. There are a number of things that we could choose out of this parable to differentiate between the groups, but the dividing line is given to us by the Lord. He said to those who did not go in with the bridegroom, "I know you not."

It is true that the oil represents the Holy Spirit; every true believer is indwelt by the Holy Spirit. It is also true that God calls believers wise and the unbelieving foolish. It is true that the wise virgins could not give the foolish virgins their oil; they had to get it for themselves. We cannot give salvation to others. Each person has to get it for himself by trusting Christ as Savior. But the most definitive thing about these virgins is given to us in the twelfth verse where he said, *"I know you not."*

How many people in professing Christendom go through the motions, attend the church services, carry Bibles, and sing the songs, but do not know the Lord? They may have grown up in Christian homes, may have memorized Scripture, may have a place of service in the church, but the most tragic of all things is when the Lord says, *"I know you not."* This means that they have never been born into God's family.

In Matthew 25:41 we find what may be the saddest verse in the entire Bible. The Lord said, *"Then shall he say also unto them on the left hand, Depart from me, ye cursed, into everlasting fire, prepared for the devil and his angels."*

Can you imagine people sincerely believing that they are going to heaven and being told, *"Depart from me"*? In this parable about the virgins, there were people who thought they were ready, but the Lord declares of them here, *"I know you not"* and they did not get in. There is nothing on earth that deserves more attention than the matter of making sure we are children of God. Everything depends on this–heaven or hell, Christ or a Christless eternity, endless joy or constant, conscious, unending suffering. It all hinges on knowing Jesus Christ. The difference between these two groups was that He said He knew one group, and of the other group He said, *"I know you not."*

There is nothing on earth that deserves more attention than the matter of making sure we are children of God.

Does the Lord know you? Does the Lord know you to be one of His own? If you have the slightest doubt, settle it! Be sure. We can be sure of our salvation because God's Word is true.

THE DOOR WAS SHUT

There is coming a moment when all opportunity for salvation will be over. The Bible says that while these virgins slept, they heard a sound. The cry came, "The bridegroom cometh!" They tried to prepare for His coming. They had lamps, but without the oil they had no light. The wise virgins sent the five foolish to buy oil. The Bible says that while they were trying to buy it, the door was shut.

The Parables of Jesus

The Word of God says in verse ten, *"And while they went to buy, the bridegroom came; and they that were ready went in with him to the marriage: and the door was shut."* There is such finality in this statement. The door was shut. It was over.

We are people of great privilege. When people start thinking about what they are going to cut out of their lives, they often start cutting out God or what they do for God. We need to be very careful, because our opportunity does not last forever. I will preach my last sermon someday. We will sing our last song. We will have our last opportunity to speak to others about the name of the Lord Jesus.

When the door is shut, and we are gone, we will leave behind a doomed world.

Once we have repented of our sin and trusted the Lord as our Savior, we should do what we can to lead others to trust the Lord as their Savior. When Jesus Christ comes again, our opportunity will be over. If we have not trusted in Him for salvation, the door of opportunity will be shut forever, and those of us who have trusted Him as our Savior will lose our opportunity to serve Him on earth.

In John 10:7 the Bible says, *"Then said Jesus unto them again, Verily, verily, I say unto you, I am the door of the sheep."* The Lord Jesus is the door! This door is open now; He waits with open arms, saying, *"Come unto me, all ye that labour and are heavy laden, and I will give you rest"* (Matthew 11:28). This door says, *"Come unto me,"* and *"For whosoever shall call upon the name of the Lord shall be saved"* (Romans 10:13).

This door waits with arms wide open, saying, *"For God so loved the world, that he gave his only begotten Son, that whosoever believeth in him should not perish, but have everlasting life"* (John 3:16).

In Revelation 4:1 the Bible says, *"After this I looked, and, behold, a door was opened in heaven."* How long is this door open? Jesus Christ has had the door of salvation open, but there will come a moment when the door of heaven will open, and the Lord will say, "Come up." The Lord Jesus Christ will rapture us to be with Him, and in the twinkling of an eye, it will be over. Surely all of us know that the return of Christ is much closer than it has ever been.

In this parable, our Lord teaches the great truth that what we do must be done now. We must act quickly. The opportunity does not last very long.

My first pastor, who is still faithfully serving the Lord, said to me when I was eighteen years old, "If you are going to do something for God with your life, start doing it now."

If you really felt in your heart that the door was going to be shut, how many of you who are not already serving Christ would be busy for God? How many of you who have made excuses would be serving the Lord now? There is an old hymn by Grace Adkins entitled "I'll Wish I Had Given Him More." The chorus says,

> More, so much more,
>
> More of my life than I e'er gave before.
>
> By and by when I look on His face,
>
> I'll wish I had given Him more.

How serious would you be about the things of God if you really believed that the door was going to shut? When the door is shut, and we are gone, we will leave behind a doomed world.

THE DESTINY WAS SETTLED

When the door was shut, the destiny of the foolish virgins was settled. The Bible says in Matthew 25:13, *"Watch therefore, for ye know neither the day nor the hour wherein the Son of man cometh."* We are to watch because when that day and hour comes, destiny is settled.

Our hope is not in the Second Coming of Christ, but in the Christ of the Second Coming.

How do we prepare? How do we watch? Does God expect that we will go without sleep and sit somewhere until we absolutely cannot hold our eyes open any longer? Is this how we watch?

There is a purifying hope in the Christian life when we are looking for and loving the Lord's appearing. God's Word says in I John 3:3, *"And every man that hath this hope in him purifieth himself, even as he is pure."* You may say, "What about all these centuries that have passed, and He still has not come?" That just proves all the more that He is coming soon. Our hope is not in the Second Coming of Christ, but in the Christ of the Second Coming; it is not so much our disappearing as it is His appearing.

The Bible says in I Peter 3:14-15,

> *But and if ye suffer for righteousness' sake, happy are ye: and be not afraid of their terror, neither be troubled; but sanctify the Lord God in your hearts: and be ready always to give an answer to every man that asketh you a reason of the hope that is in you with meekness and fear.*

How do we get ready for the Lord's return? Someone may say, "I have asked God to forgive my sin; by faith I have trusted the Lord Jesus as my Savior, and I believe the Lord is coming again. Is that all of it?" No. If that were all of it, I could have stopped many years ago. When a Christian does not do anything to try to get anyone else to Christ, I have trouble believing he really thinks his Lord is coming again.

The Lord Jesus said, *"Watch therefore, for ye know neither the day nor the hour wherein the Son of man cometh."* The way we are to watch is by living for Him and loving His appearing on a daily basis. I believe with all of my heart that there are a handful of things that define the church. One of the main things on that list is our conviction about the return of Jesus Christ. It gives urgency, holiness, purity, and soul-winning zeal. These things are results of the proper teaching of the Lord's return and the conviction we hold about the Lord's return. He is coming again. This affects the way I live and respond to things. It has a dynamic effect on the way I teach and preach. It has an effect on what I believe about problems and solutions. It is not just a doctrine that someone teaches us, and we say, "That's good information." It produces a change in our lives personally. The Lord is coming.

> *The way we are to watch is by living for Him and loving His appearing on a daily basis.*

Notice carefully where the Lord Jesus placed the emphasis. When He finished this parable, He said, *"Watch therefore, for ye know neither the day nor the hour wherein the Son of man cometh."* We must heed His command and be ready for the coming of the Lord Jesus Christ. Are you watching for His return? Look for and love His appearing!

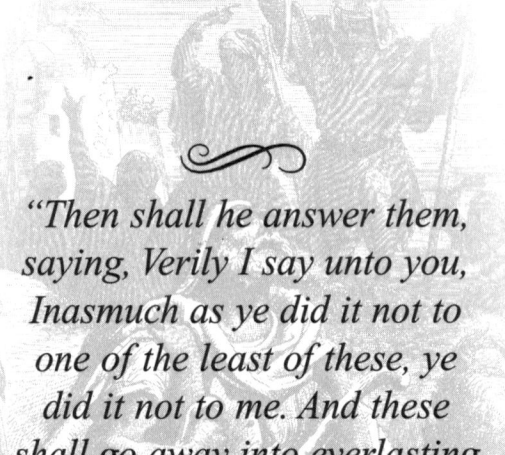

"Then shall he answer them, saying, Verily I say unto you, Inasmuch as ye did it not to one of the least of these, ye did it not to me. And these shall go away into everlasting punishment: but the righteous into life eternal."

Matthew 25:45-46

Chapter Two

THE SHEEP AND THE GOATS

he Lord Jesus Christ was the most powerful of all preachers. He gave many discourses. The parable of the sheep and the goats is part of the Olivet Discourse, one of the greatest portions of Scripture. There are two verses in this passage that we call parabolic verses. When we move beyond these verses, we read clear statements about judgment that are not in the form of a parable.

The Bible says in Matthew 25:31-46,

> *When the Son of man shall come in his glory, and all the holy angels with him, then shall he sit upon the throne of his glory: and before him shall be gathered all nations: and he shall separate them one from another, as a shepherd divideth his sheep from the goats: and he shall set the sheep on his right hand, but the goats on the left. Then shall the*

The Parables of Jesus

King say unto them on his right hand, Come, ye blessed of my Father, inherit the kingdom prepared for you from the foundation of the world: for I was an hungred, and ye gave me meat: I was thirsty, and ye gave me drink: I was a stranger, and ye took me in: naked, and ye clothed me: I was sick, and ye visited me: I was in prison, and ye came unto me. Then shall the righteous answer him, saying, Lord, when saw we thee an hungred, and fed thee? or thirsty, and gave thee drink? When saw we thee a stranger, and took thee in? or naked, and clothed thee? Or when saw we thee sick, or in prison, and came unto thee? And the King shall answer and say unto them, Verily I say unto you, Inasmuch as ye have done it unto one of the least of these my brethren, ye have done it unto me. Then shall he say also unto them on the left hand, Depart from me, ye cursed, into everlasting fire, prepared for the devil and his angels: for I was an hungred, and ye gave me no meat; I was thirsty, and ye gave me no drink: I was a stranger, and ye took me not in: naked, and ye clothed me not: sick, and in prison, and ye visited me not. Then shall they also answer him, saying, Lord, when saw we thee an hungred, or athirst, or a stranger, or naked, or sick, or in prison, and did not minister unto thee? Then shall he answer them, saying, Verily I say unto you, Inasmuch as ye did it not to one of the least of these, ye did it not to me. And these shall go away into everlasting punishment: but the righteous into life eternal.

The Lord Jesus Christ walked out of the temple, pronouncing God's judgment upon it. There were huge stones in the temple that were forty feet long, twenty feet wide, and twelve feet high–as big as some dwelling places. The Lord said that these stones would not

The Sheep and the Goats

be left one upon another. His hearers were astonished, and they asked the Lord, *"When shall these things be? What shall be the sign of Thy coming and of the end of the world?"* These three questions were given one after the other. As our Lord began to answer these questions in chapters twenty-four and twenty-five of Matthew, He taught specific things.

In Matthew 24:4-26 our Lord speaks first of the Tribulation. The Tribulation period will last for seven years. This time will begin immediately after the church is raptured. There will be two equal periods of three-and-a-half years, the last of which is referred to as the Great Tribulation. The center of the Tribulation will be marked by the *"abomination of desolation"* when the Antichrist breaks his covenant with the Jews, and they flee and hide themselves.

During the Tribulation, 144,000 flaming Jewish evangelists will preach the gospel. This period will be marked not only by the judgment of God on the earth, but also by a great worldwide revival with multitudes coming to Christ for salvation because of the preaching of these evangelists. It will also be a time when the Jews will be prepared for the Second Coming of the Lord Jesus Christ.

God's Word says in Matthew 24:15-16, *"When ye therefore shall see the abomination of desolation, spoken of by Daniel the prophet, stand in the holy place, (whoso readeth, let him understand:) then let them which be in Judaea flee into the mountains."*

The Bible tells of the Jews fleeing from the wrath of the Antichrist. Daniel 11:41 tells of one small piece of property that will escape the domination of the Antichrist. With the boundaries of this property described for us in Daniel 11:41, we recognize the location as the land of Jordan. This is why so many Bible teachers believe that the Jews shall flee to the place called Petra and will be kept there while hiding from the Antichrist. As they go throughout the world preaching the everlasting gospel of our Savior, they will be befriended, helped, visited, ministered to, and foremost, their message will be believed. This has everything to do with the parable we are studying in Matthew chapter twenty-five.

The second thing we see in this Olivet Discourse is found in Matthew 24:27-30. Here we find the mention of the Second Coming of Christ to the earth. In verse thirty-one, we see the third thing, the regathering of Israel. The Jews have been scattered, and there will be a regathering of the Jews.

In the twenty-fifth chapter, verses one through thirty, we find God's judgment on Israel. Then we come to Matthew 25:31-46, where we find God's judgment on the Gentile nations. This brings us to the parable we are studying.

The Gentile nations which will be judged during this particular judgment, referred to as the judgment of the sheep and goats, will be the nations which come through the Tribulation. We believe in the pretribulational, premillennial return of Jesus Christ. We find evidence in Scripture that the church is not going through the Tribulation. We are delivered from the wrath to come. This is one of the reasons why we should be glad we are saved. However, there are Gentile nations which will be going through the Tribulation period.

THE TIME OF THIS JUDGMENT

The Bible says in Matthew 25:31-34,

> *When the Son of man shall come in his glory, and all the holy angels with him, then shall he sit upon the throne of his glory: and before him shall be gathered all nations: and he shall separate them one from another, as a shepherd divideth his sheep from the goats: and he shall set the sheep on his right hand, but the goats on the left. Then shall the King say unto them on his right hand, Come, ye blessed of my*

The Sheep and the Goats

Father, inherit the kingdom prepared for you from the foundation of the world.

The expression *"all nations"* found in verse thirty-two is speaking of the Gentile nations. Notice the word *"sheep"* and the word *"goats."* The sheep are individuals in these Gentile nations who believe on the Lord Jesus Christ and are saved. The goats are individuals in these nations who do not believe on the Lord Jesus Christ and take the mark of the beast.

Notice the word *"king"* in verse thirty-four. Also notice the word *"kingdom."* If He is the king, He has a throne. The throne is the throne of His father David. Christ is seated at the right hand of God the Father at the throne in heaven, but He is going to have an earthly throne when He rules and reigns for one thousand years upon this earth. Then in verse forty the Bible says, *"And the King shall answer and say unto them, Verily I say unto you, Inasmuch as ye have done it unto one of the least of these my brethren."* The brethren are the Jews.

This judgment will take place at the end of the Tribulation. All human government will be ended. God will begin His government, His rule and reign on the earth, in the millennial reign of Christ. At the end of the battles that make up Armageddon, after the armies of the Antichrist have been defeated, this judgment will occur. After this judgment, the saved will enter into the millennial kingdom.

Now, let us back up for a moment. The next thing to take place on God's calendar is the coming of the Lord for His own, the church. We refer to this as the Rapture. In a moment, in the twinkling of an eye, the Lord Jesus is going to come for His own. The trumpet is going to sound, and those of us who are alive will be changed in that moment and will be caught up to be with our Lord. Those Christians who have died, whose bodies are buried, will be resurrected with a redeemed body.

The Parables of Jesus

The body will come out of the grave like the glorified body of Jesus Christ. I do not believe that one speck of dust will be moved or one blade of grass will be brushed aside, because the molecular structure of that body will be like the structure of the resurrected body of the Lord Jesus. Remember that Christ walked through closed doors. Those bodies will come up out of the grave, resurrected and redeemed. People may say, "What is so important about the body?" God is not finished with it. What is so important about the bodily resurrection of Jesus Christ? The Bible says He came forth bodily. When He came forth bodily, He came forth with the promise that we shall have a new body like His resurrected body. Those of us who are alive will be changed in a moment, in the twinkling of an eye, to be caught up to be with the Lord.

> *At the conclusion of the Tribulation, the Lord Jesus Christ will come to execute judgment upon this unbelieving world.*

We are going to stand before the judgment seat of Christ, but on the earth, the world continues. The earth will enter into the Tribulation period. At the conclusion of the Tribulation, the Lord Jesus Christ will come to execute judgment upon this unbelieving world.

In Joel 3:11-16 the Bible says,

> *Assemble yourselves, and come, all ye heathen, and gather yourselves together round about: thither cause thy mighty ones to come down, O LORD. Let the heathen be wakened, and come up to the valley of Jehoshaphat: for there will I sit to judge all the heathen round about. Put ye in the sickle, for the harvest is ripe: come, get you down; for the press is full, the fats overflow; for their wickedness is great. Multitudes, multitudes in the valley of decision: for*

The Sheep and the Goats

the day of the LORD is near in the valley of decision. The sun and the moon shall be darkened, and the stars shall withdraw their shining. The LORD also shall roar out of Zion, and utter his voice from Jerusalem; and the heavens and the earth shall shake: but the LORD will be the hope of his people, and the strength of the children of Israel.

The Bible says in Zechariah 14:4, *"And his feet shall stand in that day upon the mount of Olives..."* Remember that when the Lord Jesus comes for His church in the Rapture, He does not come to the earth; we are caught up to be with Him in the clouds. All the saved will hear the trumpet and will disappear. All the bodies of the saved will be resurrected. However, when He comes seven years later in His Revelation, every eye shall see Him, and His feet will touch the Mount of Olives. When this happens, the Bible says, *"...and the mount of Olives shall cleave in the midst thereof toward the east and toward the west, and there shall be a very great valley; and half of the mountain shall remove toward the north, and half of it toward the south."*

This valley is not there at the present moment, but when His feet touch the Mount of Olives, that great valley will be formed by the cleaving of the Mount of Olives. We believe that this is where the judgment of the Gentile nations will take place. This judgment will be at the end of the Tribulation period.

Think of the scene that unfolds here. The nations of the world which are alive at the end of the Tribulation will be brought before the King of the earth, the Lord Jesus Christ, as He sits on His throne in Jerusalem. Those of us who are saved will be there. We will enter the millennial kingdom at that time, and we will see who was saved out of the Tribulation.

The Parables of Jesus

The Testimony of Belief

In Matthew chapter twenty-five, we find a wonderful passage about how believers behave. They have a testimony, not just with their mouths, but by the way they live. During the Tribulation, it is going to cost more to be a believer than at any other time. People who are not believers will take the mark of the beast. The true believers will not take the mark of the beast. They will suffer, and many will die for their faith.

The Bible says in Matthew 25:32, *"And before him shall be gathered all nations: and he shall separate them one from another, as a shepherd divideth his sheep from the goats."* This is the parabolic form of this teaching. He is comparing this judgment to the way a shepherd divides the sheep to one side and the goats to the other. He says in Matthew 25:33-34, *"And he shall set the sheep on his right hand, but the goats on the left. Then shall the King say unto them on his right hand, Come, ye blessed of my Father, inherit the kingdom prepared for you from the foundation of the world."*

Those who were listening were surprised when Christ said in verses thirty-five through forty,

> *For I was an hungred, and ye gave me meat: I was thirsty, and ye gave me drink: I was a stranger, and ye took me in: naked, and ye clothed me: I was sick, and ye visited me: I was in prison, and ye came unto me. Then shall the righteous answer him, saying, Lord, when saw we thee an hungred, and fed thee? or thirsty, and gave thee drink? When saw we thee a stranger, and took thee in? or naked, and clothed thee? Or when saw we thee sick, or in prison, and came unto thee? And the King shall answer and say unto them, Verily I say unto you, Inasmuch as ye have*

The Sheep and the Goats

done it unto one of the least of these my brethren, ye have done it unto me.

Verse thirty-seven says, *"Then shall the righteous answer him."* I am glad the Lord gave us this statement. He speaks of the righteous, those who have been made righteous by the imputed righteousness of Jesus Christ. Their behavior testified that they were believers.

Nations cannot feed, visit, or clothe people. The Lord is speaking of individuals in those nations, those Gentiles who are brought before the Lord. They are going to give evidence of whether or not they are saved by the way they respond to the Jews and what they do to help these Jews who are hiding from the Antichrist.

Do you remember the Old Testament story of Rahab the harlot? Rahab lived in the ancient city of Jericho. When the spies sent by Joshua came to Jericho, she hid them. She proved by her actions that she believed the Lord. She was justified before God by her faith and justified before men by her works. Her works gave evidence of her faith. The Bible says in James 2:25, *"Likewise also was not Rahab the harlot justified by works, when she had received the messengers, and had sent them out another way?"* She proved she was a believer by the way she responded in this time of crisis.

During the Tribulation period, people are not saved by their works, because people are never saved by their works. They are only saved by the grace of God through faith. However, their works give evidence that they are saved, just as our works give evidence that we are God's children. This makes me think about many people who say they are Christians yet give no evidence that they are saved. It is one thing to sin as a Christian. It is another thing to enjoy sin and continue in that sin and never do anything about it. If a man has been born again, he will give evidence of this by the way he behaves. The weak, costless Christianity that is being promoted in this apostate age is not the Christianity of the Bible.

The Parables of Jesus

We prove every day of our lives whether or not we are believers by the way we respond to things. We prove this to an unbelieving world by our honesty and integrity, decency, God-fearing attitude, and virtue. This does not mean there is anyone who is perfect, but when God deals with us, and we know we have sinned, we prove we are saved by repenting of our sin and asking God to forgive us and cleanse us.

I was just a boy when I was saved. In my early teens I got away from the Lord and brought reproach to the name of Christ. No one would have thought I was a Christian. For a few months in my life, I did things a Christian should not have done. What took me just a few months to do took years to overcome. Thank God that *"for peace I had great bitterness: but thou hast in love to my soul delivered it from the pit of corruption: for thou hast cast all my sins behind thy back"* (Isaiah 38:17). Jesus Christ is a wonderful Savior! He forgives and forgets. He always remembers to forget. I do not have to face those sins ever again. They are forgiven under the blood of the Lord Jesus.

The weak, costless Christianity that is being promoted in this apostate age is not the Christianity of the Bible.

None of us have the testimony we should, but we must guard the testimony we do have. This is very important. The Bible says, *"A good name is rather to be chosen than great riches"* (Proverbs 22:1). Some people give up their testimony for riches.

As we look at this particular passage as it relates to the Tribulation, the saved give testimony in that awful crisis time in human history. The Bible says there has never been anything like it, and there shall never be anything like it again, yet these Christians live for Christ during this time. Their living for Him proves that they know Him. May God help us in this weak age in which we live to have boldness for our Savior.

THE TRAGEDY OF UNBELIEF

There is nothing as tragic as unbelief. I hear some people say, "If there were no heaven and no hell, it would still be wonderful to be a Christian." I believe that, though I do not use that illustration. There is no sense in hypothetically saying, "If there were no heaven or hell," because there is a heaven and there is a hell.

Unbelief is tragic. Unbelievers lose now, though they think they win; they walk in darkness now, though they think it is light. There is a difference between believers and unbelievers in this life. However, the greatest difference between believers and unbelievers is not in life; it is in death and eternity.

The Bible says in Matthew 25:40-41,

> *And the King shall answer and say unto them, Verily I say unto you, Inasmuch as ye have done it unto one of the least of these my brethren, ye have done it unto me. Then shall he say also unto them on the left hand, Depart from me, ye cursed, into everlasting fire, prepared for the devil and his angels.*

Lost people are going to go where the Devil is going. God help us. If this is true, why do we not do more to win the lost? If we love the Lord Jesus as we say we love Him, why do we not talk about Him more than we do? The use of our time testifies that our priorities are not what they should be. There is a world without Christ headed to hell.

The Lord Jesus said in verses forty-two through forty-five,

> *For I was an hungred, and ye gave me no meat; I was thirsty, and ye gave me no drink: I was a*

> *stranger, and ye took me not in: naked, and ye clothed me not: sick, and in prison, and ye visited me not. Then shall they also answer him, saying, Lord, when saw we thee an hungred, or athirst, or a stranger, or naked, or sick, or in prison, and did not minister unto thee? Then shall he answer them, saying, Verily I say unto you, Inasmuch as ye did it not to one of the least of these, ye did it not to me.*

During the Tribulation period, people will have opportunity to help and minister to these Jews. It is not the helping and ministering to them that gets them saved, it is helping and ministering to these persecuted Jews that proves they have trusted in Christ. Because others do not minister to the Jews, they give evidence that they are unbelievers. The tragedy of unbelief is found in verse forty-six, *"And these shall go away into everlasting punishment: but the righteous into life eternal."*

There is nothing more tragic than someone dying and going to hell. We should speak out against sin. My heart hurts as I think of my generation walking in darkness. We are living in a biblically illiterate world. As Americans, we stand and pledge allegiance to "one nation under God" when we know that this nation is living in a post-Christian era. Like nations of decline in Europe which have gone from Christianity to atheism, we have moved through Christianity in America to a post-Christian era. This is showing up everywhere. Bible-believing Christians are becoming more of a minority with every passing day. We cannot bury our heads in the sand and try to escape the reality of it.

People agree that this is tragic, but what can we do? We can begin to view this nation and our world as a sinking ship. The best thing we can do is try to get as many people in the lifeboats as we possibly can. By this I mean that we need to declare the gospel to as many as we possibly can.

The Sheep and the Goats

I made a promise when I was eighteen years old. After hearing a man say that D. L. Moody tried to witness to at least one unsaved person every day, I came forward in the service and I said, "I want to do that. God, help me to do that." The Lord reminds me often of that commitment.

There is nothing more tragic than someone dying and going to hell.

We are to know Him, to love Him, to adore Him, to worship Him, to fellowship with Him, to walk with Him, and to talk with Him. All these things must be priorities. But we are also to tell people about Him. We need to say, "Lord, please help me while there is time to be the witness I should be." May God help us to realize the tragedy of unbelief and let us seek to win the lost to Christ.

"No man also seweth a piece of new cloth on an old garment: else the new piece that filled it up taketh away from the old, and the rent is made worse."

Mark 2:21

Chapter Three

THE NEW CLOTH ON AN OLD GARMENT

hristianity cannot be reduced to a ritual. There is no way to reduce the Christian faith to "dos" and "don'ts." Many who followed Christ during His earthly ministry had the idea that the Lord came simply to add something to the religion they already had; they thought that something was missing from Judaism to make it what it should be. They were accustomed to a religion of mourning and fasting, but now they witnessed laughter and feasting. They had instructed people to live right, yet Christ ate with publicans and sinners, the outcasts of society. They did not understand this. In the context of their confusion, the Lord said in Mark 2:21-22,

> *No man also seweth a piece of new cloth on an old garment: else the new piece that filled it up taketh away from the old, and the rent is made*

> worse. And no man putteth new wine into old bottles: else the new wine doth burst the bottles, and the wine is spilled, and the bottles will be marred: but new wine must be put into new bottles.

When we come to the Gospel according to Mark, in chapter two, we find the Lord Jesus Christ in Capernaum, coming face to face with Levi, called Matthew. Levi was a publican who sat at the receipt of custom. As the Lord Jesus spoke to him, Levi left his position at the receipt of custom and followed the Savior. He was so excited about trusting Christ that he had a feast for the Lord at his home. He invited others to come and dine with him. As he did, the Pharisees heard of it. They thought, "Jesus, this great teacher, is with the worst people in society."

They did not go to Christ, they went to His disciples. The Bible says in Mark 2:16-20,

> And when the scribes and Pharisees saw him eat with publicans and sinners, they said unto his disciples, How is it that he eateth and drinketh with publicans and sinners? When Jesus heard it, he saith unto them, They that are whole have no need of the physician, but they that are sick: I came not to call the righteous, but sinners to repentance. And the disciples of John and of the Pharisees used to fast: and they come and say unto him, Why do the disciples of John and of the Pharisees fast, but thy disciples fast not? And Jesus said unto them, Can the children of the bridechamber fast, while the bridegroom is with them? as long as they have the bridegroom with them, they cannot fast. But the days will come, when the bridegroom will be taken away from them, and then shall they fast in those days.

The New Cloth on an Old Garment

The Lord said, "As long as the bridegroom is with the people in the bridechamber, they will respond to the bridegroom. They will be excited and filled with laughter and joy because they are with the bridegroom."

Jesus Christ is the Bridegroom. He said, *"Can the children of the bridechamber fast, while the bridegroom is with them?"* The truth is, He has never left us nor forsaken us, so we should always be rejoicing. He promised us in Hebrews 13:5, *"I will never leave thee, nor forsake thee."*

I doubt if this younger generation has any idea at all about what it means to patch a piece of clothing. The idea is that new cloth attached to an old garment will not work; it will tear the old. The new wine put in an old bottle will not work; it will burst the bottle.

Our Lord declared that He did not come to patch up an old religion. He did not come simply to add something to Judaism. Christ does not work that way. Our Lord does not do "patchwork." Many people, when it comes to their religion, are attempting to patch up or to add something else to please God. They think they will finally get the formula exactly as it should be, and when they do, things will go well. The Christian faith is not a system of works in an effort to please God. It is something new.

> *The Christian faith is not a system of works in an effort to please God. It is something new.*

WE HAVE A NEW COVENANT

The Bible says in Matthew twenty-six that we have a new covenant relationship with God. Matthew 26:27-28 says, *"And he took the cup, and gave thanks, and gave it to them, saying, Drink ye*

The Parables of Jesus

all of it; for this is my blood of the new testament, which is shed for many for the remission of sins."

The new cloth is Christianity and the old cloth is Judaism. The new wine is Christianity and the old bottles are Judaism. Christianity is not patching up something old with something new; it is entirely new. As believers, we enter into this covenant.

How important is this to understand? It concerns our soul's salvation; this is how important it is. The Bible says in John 17:1-5,

> *These words spake Jesus, and lifted up his eyes to heaven, and said, Father, the hour is come; glorify thy Son, that thy Son also may glorify thee: as thou hast given him power over all flesh, that he should give eternal life to as many as thou hast given him. And this is life eternal, that they might know thee the only true God, and Jesus Christ, whom thou hast sent. I have glorified thee on the earth: I have finished the work which thou gavest me to do. And now, O Father, glorify thou me with thine own self with the glory which I had with thee before the world was.*

Our Lord does not do "patchwork."

The Lord Jesus did not say, "Before I came." He said, *"Before the world was."* We read on in verses six and seven,

> *I have manifested thy name unto the men which thou gavest me out of the world: thine they were, and thou gavest them me; and they have kept thy word. Now they have known that all things whatsoever thou hast given me are of thee.*

The New Cloth on an Old Garment

What is this covenant? Some people who are Christians have the idea that the covenant we enter into is a covenant that we have with God. No, it is a covenant that God the Father has made with God the Son.

God the Son came to earth and bled and died on the cross in obedience to God the Father. God the Son, in the predetermined counsel of Almighty God, willingly determined He would come to earth and bleed and die for our sins. This is why the Bible says in Revelation 13:8 that He is the Lamb of God *"slain from the foundation of the world."* This is why the Bible says in Isaiah 53:5, hundreds of years before Christ went to Calvary, that He was *"wounded for our transgressions, he was bruised for our iniquities: the chastisement of our peace was upon Him."*

God the Father demanded justice and provided mercy.

These verbs are all past tense because in the mind of God, it was a settled fact that Jesus Christ would shed His blood on the cross for our sins. There is a covenant relationship made with God the Father and God the Son that if God the Son would bleed and die for our sins, God the Father would give God the Son all who come to God by faith.

We do not have to do something to remain saved. We do not have to please God to stay in His family. God the Father has presented each of us to His dear Son. We have been made gifts to God. The Lord Jesus said in John 17:6, *"I have manifested thy name unto the men which thou gavest me out of the world: thine they were, and thou gavest them me; and they have kept thy word."* To whom was He talking? He was talking to God the Father. Through that blood covenant, God the Father has given us to God the Son. We cannot lose ourselves. In fact, we can never be lost again because He will never lose us. Our salvation is a new cloth; it is a new wine; it is a new covenant. As believers, we have entered into the covenant that God the Father has with God the Son.

I am glad I belong to the Lord. This is a new covenant sealed in His blood. Would you like to know if God accepted the blood of Christ for my soul's salvation? Yes, this is evidenced in the fact that the payment was made in the blood of Christ and the receipt for the payment was given by the bodily resurrection of Jesus Christ from the grave.

God the Father demanded justice and provided mercy. He accepted the sacrifice of His Son and gave evidence that He accepted that sacrifice by the resurrection of the Lord Jesus Christ from the dead. It is a new covenant.

WE HAVE A NEW COMMUNION

We commune with God the Father through God the Son, and we fellowship in this communion with one another, as brothers and sisters in Christ. Let us look at what the apostle Paul wrote in I Corinthians 10:16-17. The Bible says,

> *The cup of blessing which we bless, is it not the communion of the blood of Christ? The bread which we break, is it not the communion of the body of Christ? For we being many are one bread, and one body: for we are all partakers of that one bread.*

This is essential in order for believers to live the way they should live. I may have a problem with you. If I do, I need to remember that I have a new communion with God the Father. I must stay right with God so that I can stay right with you. I must fellowship with God so that I am able to fellowship with you.

If you and I do not fellowship together as we should, it is evidence that one of us is not communing with God as he should. If you and I cannot agree as Christians, then something is not right in my fellowship with the Lord.

The New Cloth on an Old Garment

We have entered into Christ, not some sort of performance. We are part of His body. By His shed blood, we are part of His body and this communion we now enjoy. God has a family, and we are a part of His family. Hebrews 2:10 says, *"For it became him, for whom are all things, and by whom are all things, in bringing many sons unto glory, to make the captain of their salvation perfect through sufferings."* He did this through His work on Calvary. If you declare that you are a part of His family, then I am your brother in the Lord. Brothers and sisters in the Lord not only should, but can in every circumstance as they trust God to enable them, walk together and be agreed. We have a new communion. It is something that is entirely possible, and there is no excuse for us not to get along and do God's work the way it should be done because we have this new communion.

> *If you and I do not fellowship together as we should, it is evidence that one of us is not communing with God as he should.*

My first experience in a church where I sought to serve the Lord was in a place where one brother sat on one side of the auditorium and the other brother sat on the opposite side of the auditorium. They both claimed to be Christians, and they both held responsible positions in the church, yet they never spoke to one another. They came into the church without speaking to one another, and they left without speaking to one another. They made sure that they never crossed each other's path. It became a humorous thing to some people. But how tragic for two brothers–related by physical birth and spiritual birth–to behave in such a disobedient way.

I think that there is a God in heaven who wanted to do things in that church, and those men, who are both now in the presence of God, are going to have to answer to God for harming the blessed fellowship of that ministry. God could not do all He desired to do because of the sin of those men. I believe with all my heart that we are going to answer to God for what we would not allow God to do because of our refusal to be right with Him and with one another. This is a serious matter.

The Christian life is not a patchwork. We have a new communion. You and I can enter into the presence of God through what the Lord Jesus Christ has done for us through His death, burial, and resurrection. We approach the throne of God on the merits of our Lord and Savior Jesus Christ.

WE ARE NEW CREATURES

The third thing we understand from this parable is that we are new creatures. We are new creations, not a patchwork job. The Bible says in II Corinthians 5:14-17,

> *For the love of Christ constraineth us; because we thus judge, that if one died for all, then were all dead: and that he died for all, that they which live should not henceforth live unto themselves, but unto him which died for them, and rose again. Wherefore henceforth know we no man after the flesh: yea, though we have known Christ after the flesh, yet now henceforth know we him no more. Therefore if any man be in Christ, he is a new creature: old things are passed away; behold, all things are become new.*

This expression *"new creature,"* meaning "new creation," is the same expression we find when God made the world. Out of nothing, God spoke something into existence. God did not find something in me and make it blossom and grow. I was dead in my trespasses and sins. We believe that death does not mean that we are totally unable to respond to God. We do believe that we are dead in our trespasses

The New Cloth on an Old Garment

and sins, but we can still respond to God of our own will and volition. When God dealt with us by His Holy Spirit, He drew us to Himself. When we were born into the family of God, we had a new birth. We are now new creations. Salvation is of the Lord!

God did not patch something inside of me. He did not say, "There is something in that fellow. He is really a good boy and I am going to bring it out of him." No, this is not the way God does His work in salvation. God brings about something altogether new. Just like God spoke the world into existence from nothing, God made us new creatures. He gave us new birth. He made us Christians. It did not come from something in us. Salvation is completely of the Lord. My sinful condition separated me from God. We are regenerated by His power.

I am a new man, and I do not need to try to reform myself. The Bible says in Romans 12:1-2,

> *I beseech you therefore, brethren, by the mercies of God, that ye present your bodies a living sacrifice, holy, acceptable unto God, which is your reasonable service. And be not conformed to this world: but be ye transformed by the renewing of your mind, that ye may prove what is that good, and acceptable, and perfect, will of God.*

The Bible uses the word *"transformed."* It does not say "reformed." The Christian life is not some outward reformation. It is not some play on the stage of life, trying to pretend to be what I should be and what you expect me to be. It is not putting a piece of new cloth on an old garment. The Christian life is all new. I am a new creation. It is God doing something in me and through me, transforming my life. This is the Christian life.

You may think, "I cannot live the way God wants me to live." Yes, you can. *"I can do all things through Christ which strengtheneth me"* (Philippians 4:13). Do you realize how many times we try to turn over a new leaf? We try to work things out. We try to go another way, turn another page, seek other counsel. When we have Christ in us, we are new creations, and He enables us. He lives in us, He indwells us, He helps us, He transforms us.

I am so tired of struggling with "patching up my life." God does not want to do that. You may say, "I have just fallen into the same old trap. I am going to conquer it one of these days." You cannot conquer it. All you can do is die to self and ask Christ to conquer it. You may say, "I am going to finally get over this." No, you are going to lug that old nature around until the day you die, and so am I. We do not conquer it. We do not squeeze into some sort of form we can control and handle. This is not the way to live the Christian life. This is patchwork. Victory is not in the repression of sin; it is in the confession of sin.

The way God sees me is the way He sees His own dear Son. He sees me as a new creation.

The Jews had all the regulations and all the rituals. They had the idea that they would do one thing after another until everything lined up. If they could just add this or that, finally everything would be right. The Lord said, *"No man also seweth a piece of new cloth on an old garment...And no man putteth new wine into old bottles."* This is not what He came to do. He came to give us a new covenant, a new communion, to make of us a new creature in Christ Jesus our Lord.

I am not all I should be, but I thank God I am not what I once was. I know by His grace I can be more of what He wants me to be, not because I am able, but because He enables me. I do not need to whine and say, "I can't." I can through Him. I have a new power to do what I cannot do on my own. Someone may say, "I just can't forgive that person." No, you cannot, but Christ in you can. You may say, "I just can't get over this." No, you cannot, but Christ in you can.

The New Cloth on an Old Garment

You may say, "I just can't be faithful." No, you cannot, but Christ in you can. Many of us have no problem talking to people about God speaking the world into existence, referring to Creation with all its splendor and glory; but here He uses the same term for what He has done in us. We are a new creation.

God does not see me as a Christian that has been put together with spare parts. I am not running around with patches all over me. The way God sees me is the way He sees His own dear Son. He sees me as a new creation. The Bible declares in Romans 4:24, *"But for us also, to whom it shall be imputed, if we believe on him that raised up Jesus our Lord from the dead."* He sees me through the blood of the Lord Jesus, transformed by His mighty power. From this vantage point, I need to reckon self to be dead and allow Christ to have His way in me. I want to live that kind of Christian life. May the Lord help us all to do this.

"Which now of these three, thinkest thou, was neighbour unto him that fell among the thieves? And he said, He that shewed mercy on him. Then said Jesus unto him, Go, and do thou likewise."

Luke 10:36-37

Who Is Neighbor to Those in Need?

hen was the last time you helped someone in need? There is an expression used often in the southern states that has to do with showing kindness to others. The person who shows acts of kindness is referred to as being "neighborly." The Lord Jesus Christ was asked the question, *"Who is my neighbour?"* This question was meant to trap Him, but He responded by giving the parable of the Good Samaritan found in Luke 10:30-37,

> *And Jesus answering said, A certain man went down from Jerusalem to Jericho, and fell among thieves, which stripped him of his raiment, and wounded him, and departed, leaving him half dead. And by chance there came down a certain priest that way: and when he saw him, he passed by on the other side. And likewise a Levite, when*

he was at the place, came and looked on him, and passed by on the other side. But a certain Samaritan, as he journeyed, came where he was: and when he saw him, he had compassion on him, and went to him, and bound up his wounds, pouring in oil and wine, and set him on his own beast, and brought him to an inn, and took care of him. And on the morrow when he departed, he took out two pence, and gave them to the host, and said unto him, Take care of him; and whatsoever thou spendest more, when I come again, I will repay thee. Which now of these three, thinkest thou, was neighbour unto him that fell among the thieves? And he said, He that shewed mercy on him. Then said Jesus unto him, Go, and do thou likewise.

The Bible says in Luke 10:25, *"And, behold, a certain lawyer..."* We can refer to this man as a scribe. He was an authority in the Old Testament law. The Bible says he came to tempt Christ. He wanted to ask Christ a question, hoping to embarrass the Lord, to shame or discredit Him in the presence of others.

God's Word says in Luke 10:25-27,

> *And, behold, a certain lawyer stood up, and tempted him, saying, Master, what shall I do to inherit eternal life? He said unto him, What is written in the law? how readest thou? And he answering said, Thou shalt love the Lord thy God with all thy heart, and with all thy soul, and with all thy strength, and with all thy mind; and thy neighbour as thyself.*

The Lord said to him in verse twenty-eight, *"Thou hast answered right: this do, and thou shalt live."* The truth is that he had not done, nor would he ever do all those things. No one else who has ever lived has done all those things. No one has ever kept all the law except the Lord Jesus Christ. He is the only perfect One who ever lived. He is the only One who ever lived and did not sin.

There is no doubt that this scribe was convicted that he had not done all these things. He decided to ask Christ a question that perhaps could not be answered. To disguise his guilt and change the subject, he said to our Lord Jesus, *"And who is my neighbour?"* As Christ concludes this parable, He does not ask the same question. If you do not read carefully, it will sound like the same question.

This authority in the law asked Christ, *"Who is my neighbour?"* In other words, "To whom am I to show compassion?" The Lord asked him, in verses thirty-six and thirty-seven, *"Which now of these three, thinkest thou, was neighbour unto him that fell among the thieves? And he said, He that shewed mercy on him."*

Christ turned it completely around. He did not ask the man, "To whom are we to care for and show compassion?" (Who is my neighbor?) Instead, He asked the man, "Who showed compassion?" (Who will be a neighbor to those in need?)

THE INJURY AGAINST THE TRAVELER

Notice the crime against this traveler. The Bible says in verse thirty, *"And Jesus answering said, A certain man went down from Jerusalem to Jericho, and fell among thieves, which stripped him of his raiment, and wounded him, and departed, leaving him half dead."*

This man could well represent to us all of the human race. A certain man went down from Jerusalem, the holy city of God, down to Jericho, the city that is cursed. This tells the story of mankind in his fall from God.

The Bible says the man fell among thieves. The Bible says in John 8:44 that the Devil is a liar and a murderer. This parable is more than just a story. It pictures the fall of man and his sinful condition.

These thieves robbed the man, wounded him, and left him half dead. Note the interesting expression, *"leaving him half dead."* If he were half dead, was he going to live or was he going to die? What was going to happen to him? It would depend on the response of the person who came along and found him.

"Half dead" meant that he could either live or die. The world is half dead. Are they going to die or are they going to live? Are they going to hear of salvation in the Lord Jesus Christ? Will they be saved and forgiven and made free and alive unto God? Or are they going to die? Our responsibility is to go to them.

THE INDIFFERENCE OF THOSE PASSING BY

Those who passed by were not expected to be cold-hearted, but they were. The Bible says, *"And by chance there came down a certain priest that way..."* He had his opportunity. This was a man who made sacrifices and offerings. *"...and when he saw him, he passed by on the other side."* This priest avoided the man.

There is a particular road that goes down from Jerusalem to Jericho. It is called the Valley of the Shadow of Death. This old Roman highway snakes its way through rocky areas filled with caves and hiding places. At the time of Christ, it was a place that was notorious for robbers, thieves, and murderers. Perhaps this priest was frightened. Maybe he thought, "Someone has beaten this man and left him for dead. If I get too close and linger too long, the same could happen to me." So the priest passed by.

No amount of offering or sacrifice given could meet the need of those represented by this man. All the priests and all the offerings

Who Is Neighbor to Those in Need?

could not help them. It would take the Lamb of God, slain from the foundation of the world, to help this fallen human race.

The Bible says in verse thirty-two, *"And likewise a Levite, when he was at the place, came and looked on him, and passed by on the other side."* The Levite was a religious leader who was expected to be the kind of person who would help. He thought, "If I'm going to love my neighbor as myself, I have to know who the neighbor is. Why don't you tell me?" He was trying to justify himself.

The Lord Jesus told the man this story of the priest passing by. The priest, the one who was to stand between God and man for the people, did not care. The Levite, who witnessed sacrifices and offerings, did not care. He held a position, but he had no compassion.

THE INVOLVEMENT OF THE SAMARITAN

To mention a Samaritan in this context was like pouring salt in an open wound because the Jews hated the Samaritans, and the Samaritans hated the Jews. When the Northern Kingdom was carried captive, they fell to the Assyrian empire. Some were left behind because they were weak and feeble. Over the centuries, those Jews married Gentiles, and this mixed race inhabited the land of Samaria. All of this took place about 750 years before the coming of Christ. Around 535 B.C., when the second temple was being built, the Samaritans went down, according to the book of Ezra, and offered to help build it. Their help was refused, so they decided to build their own temple and have their own worship. The Jews had nothing to do with the Samaritans, and the Samaritans had nothing to do with the Jews.

The Lord said to this lawyer in Luke 10:33, *"But a certain Samaritan..."* I can imagine that the lawyer's eyes opened wide and his ears perked up when Christ said that. *"But a certain Samaritan as he journeyed, came where he was; and when he saw him, he had*

The Parables of Jesus

compassion on him..." No doubt, we are taking for granted that this traveler from Jerusalem to Jericho was a Jew, yet the Samaritan who knew that the Jews hated him is the only one who cared about the Jew. Even though he was hated and despised by the man who was wounded, he cared for him. What a picture of our Savior, who loves those who have no love for Him, who shows compassion to those who have no feeling of compassion or love for Him.

People who have compassion find a way to get things done.

The Bible says in verse thirty-four, *"And went to him, and bound up his wounds, pouring in oil and wine."* These are pictures of the Holy Spirit and the precious blood of Christ. This is what is necessary for our healing. The Bible says he *"set him on his own beast..."* He got off the beast and humbled himself. He gave so that this man could have what he needed. What a picture of our Savior! He came to earth, humbled Himself, and became a man without ceasing to be God. He became not just a man, but a servant, and not just a servant, but an obedient servant. He was obedient unto death, even the shameful, humiliating death of the cross. The man got down off his own beast. He walked and let the wounded man ride. He then *"brought him to an inn, and took care of him."*

Some people give money so that they do not have to give of themselves and their time. Some people give time so that they do not have to give money. Here was a man who gave time, money, and himself. He demonstrated compassion. The Word of God says in verse thirty-five, *"And on the morrow when he departed, he took out two pence, and gave them to the host, and said unto him, Take care of him: and whatsoever thou spendest more, when I come again, I will repay thee."* Everything we do in His name He will reward. He is coming again, and He will know what we have done.

Who Is Neighbor to Those in Need?

The point was made to the lawyer that the Samaritan, whom they would not expect to have compassion, had compassion. We see One greater than this Samaritan. We see our Savior who cares for the wounded, the forsaken, and the helpless.

THE INTENTION OF THE PARABLE

Christ told the story and then brought it to a conclusion. Remember, the lawyer had asked, *"Who is my neighbour?"* He was trying to justify himself. He said, "What about eternal life?" The Lord Jesus said, "What about the law? What does the law say?" The man said, "If I do everything the law says, I will have eternal life." The Lord said, "You are right." They both knew that the lawyer did not do everything the law required.

To justify himself he said, "Explain to me who my neighbor is. To whom am I responsible? To whom am I to show compassion and love? Point them out to me." We have learned that the neighbor was the person in need, but that is not the question Christ asked.

My wife and I were driving home recently when we heard an ambulance. We followed the sound of the ambulance to a dwelling right across the street from our house. We thought our neighbor, an elderly gentleman who has had heart problems, was having another serious problem. We quickly parked the car, ran up to the house, and went inside. His wife said, "He's bad. I don't know if he is going to live." We went into the bedroom where he was lying weak and feeble. The

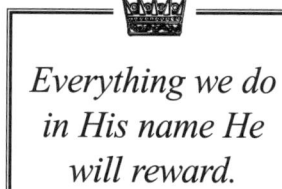

Everything we do in His name He will reward.

paramedics were attending to him. They said they would have to take him to the hospital. His wife said, "I'm just so exhausted. I just can't go." I looked at my wife and I said, "I'll go." My wife said, "We'll both go." We stayed several hours at the hospital in the emergency room. It meant so much to the fellow that I was there with him. He was in need.

We had witnessed to our neighbors, but going to the hospital for several hours was the most effective sermon we had ever preached to that family. We should have done much more. Realize that your neighbor is a person in need.

The Word of God says, *"Which now of these three, thinkest thou, was neighbour unto him that fell among the thieves?"* He did not say, "Who is the neighbor?" He said, "Who was the neighbor?" The man answered Him, *"He that shewed mercy on him. Then said Jesus unto him, Go, and do thou likewise."*

The lawyer said, "You just define to me what my responsibilities are. You line it all up for me. You tell me who I am supposed to reach. You assign me the job. Point out who the neighbor is." The Lord said, "That is not the problem. It is not that you do not know who the neighbor is. The problem is that you are not being a neighbor to those in need. The problem is not that you do not know for whom you are to care. The sin is that you do not care!"

We sit around planning and thinking, "We are going to reach our city, our community." We get our maps and ideas. We get excited and talk about all we are going to do. Finding out who we are responsible for is not a problem; the whole world is in need. The real problem is finding someone who cares enough to do what is needed.

This man who, to justify himself, said, "Spell it all out for me. Line it all up for me. Who is my neighbor? If I am going to love my neighbor as myself, which no one has ever really done, I need to know who my neighbor is." The Lord turned the whole thing around on him and said, "That is not the real need. The sin is that you do not care!"

The reason we do not do what we are commanded to do is that we do not care. We say we care. To justify ourselves, we say other things just like this man in the story. We talk about time, or place, or people,

Who Is Neighbor to Those in Need?

or lack of skills. All of this is meaningless. If we cared, we would move to action. People who have compassion find a way to get things done.

When the truth of this parable got hold of me, I became convicted of my own lack of compassion. Perhaps the Samaritan did think about who might be hiding in the rocks and that he might be attacked, yet there was something that made him go on in spite of that. The Bible says he had compassion on the man.

The problem is not that you do not know for whom you are to care. The sin is that you do not care!

We do not do what we should do because we do not care. If we cared, we would do it. The conclusion Christ brings us to is that we should not sit around trying to find out who the neighbor is. We should get on our faces and say, "Lord, my sin is that it would not make any difference if I knew who every neighbor was. I do not have the compassion it takes to do something about it." The people who will admit this are the people God will use. We need a baptism of compassion.

The man who asked what he thought were "trick" questions asked them to "compassion personified." The Lord Jesus put the sword right to his heart.

I want the Lord to help me. I want to have the mind of Christ. I want to minister with the mind of Christ. I want to live my life with the mind of Christ. Pray that God will help us not to be like the foolish scribe. If we love the Lord, we will show His compassion to others.

"Thou fool, this night thy soul shall be required of thee: then whose shall those things be, which thou hast provided?"

Luke 12:20

Chapter Five

THE RICH FOOL

hinking about the future should be a frightening experience for those who do not know the Lord Jesus Christ as their personal Savior. As we read the Bible, we find times when our Lord pulled the curtain and allowed men to look beyond this world into eternity. In the parable of the rich fool, He brought us to this heart-piercing thought using just one word.

The Bible says in Luke 12:16-20,

> *And he spake a parable unto them, saying, The ground of a certain rich man brought forth plentifully: and he thought within himself, saying, What shall I do, because I have no room where to bestow my fruits? And he said, This will I do: I will pull down my barns, and build greater; and there will I bestow all my fruits and my goods. And I will*

say to my soul, Soul, thou hast much goods laid up for many years; take thine ease, eat, drink, and be merry. But God said unto him, Thou fool, this night thy soul shall be required of thee: then whose shall those things be, which thou hast provided?

Note that one little word in the twentieth verse. It is the word *"then."* What a powerful word! The Bible says, *"But God said unto him, Thou fool, this night thy soul shall be required of thee; then whose shall those things be, which thou hast provided?" "Then"* means that all is over. Life has ended. *"Then"* speaks of the time when we come to the last chapter, the last page, the last paragraph, the last sentence, the last word. *"Then whose shall those things be, which thou hast provided?"*

All of life can be summarized with two words, *now* and *then*. There is no way to escape the fact that there will be a "then." The Bible says in Hebrews 9:27, *"And as it is appointed unto men once to die, but after this the judgment."* We should never live "now" without thinking about "then." Everything we do "now" should be done in light of "then."

Everyone of us has an inevitable meeting with God. Though some live longer than others on this earth, we all live the same length of time, because all of us will live forever either in heaven or in hell. Here and now, some will outlive others. But beyond the grave, life goes on forever.

The man in this parable was a fool. God called him a fool because he gave no attention to eternity. This man was a fool because he gave no attention to the judgment of God. He was a fool because he gave no attention to his soul. He was a fool because he did not consider the brevity of life. He was a fool because he only lived for what could be gained now. This causes me to consider my own life; you should be thinking about your life.

The Rich Fool

Do we live in light of eternity and in light of an inevitable meeting with God? Do we live in light of the certainty of death? Do we live in light of the brevity of life? If we are living only for the here and now, we are no better than the man in this parable.

On this occasion, as the Lord was speaking, there was an interruption. God took advantage of the interruption to give us this parable. The Lord Jesus was teaching the people, and the Bible says in Luke 12:13-15,

> *And one of the company said unto him, Master, speak to my brother, that he divide the inheritance with me. And he said unto him, Man, who made me a judge or a divider over you? And he said unto them, Take heed, and beware of covetousness: for a man's life consisteth not in the abundance of the things which he possesseth.*

What a statement! In my mind's eye, I can see the Lord Jesus Christ teaching and a man breaking through to get the attention of the Savior. He interrupts everything that is going on; he lifts his voice so loudly that everyone knows he is speaking to the Lord. The man says, "I have a problem. I have an inheritance that is supposed to come to me. I want you to make sure that my brother gives me my inheritance." There were people given to legal matters like that, even in our Lord's day. The Lord replies to him, *"Man, who made me a judge or a divider over you?"*

Everyone of us has an inevitable meeting with God.

Christ knew the man's heart. The problem was not the inheritance; it was the man's attitude toward possessions. We need to make sure that we get our attitudes right toward possessions. There is nothing evil or sinful about possessions. However, we can have an evil attitude toward

57

possessions by placing possessions before the Lord. We can become so comfortable with possessions that we neglect the Lord. We can give so much attention to what we get, that we forget who gave it to us. Our Lord warned here, *"Beware of covetousness."*

THE FAILURE OF SUCCESS

For most people, the two words, *failure* and *success*, do not seem to go together. In this parable we find a grand example of the failure of succeeding, because in succeeding, this man neglected God.

The Bible says in Luke 12:16, *"And he spake a parable unto them, saying, The ground of a certain rich man brought forth plentifully."* Note the word *"ground."* Christ did not say that the man worked hard to cultivate and irrigate the land. No, Christ said that the ground gave him the crop. Who formed the ground? Who made the dust of the earth? Who created the world? Who enabled the soil to produce crops? God Almighty did.

Though some live longer than others on this earth, we all live the same length of time, because all of us will live forever either in heaven or in hell.

One may say, "I am fit and I am able. I do the best I can. I work hard from daylight until dark." Well, God bless you for that kind of ingenuity and labor. But do not forget where the air you breathe comes from. The Bible declares in Deuteronomy 8:18, *"But thou shalt remember the L*ORD *thy God: for it is he that giveth thee power to get wealth."* Do not forget where you get your strength. Do not ever forget where your body came from. Inevitably, everything goes back to God Almighty. That truth is what the man in this parable neglected.

The Rich Fool

In Luke 12:16-19 the Bible says,

> *And he spake a parable unto them, saying, The ground of a certain rich man brought forth plentifully: and he thought within himself, saying, What shall I do, because I have no room where to bestow my fruits? And he said, This will I do; I will pull down my barns, and build greater; and there will I bestow all my fruits and my goods. And I will say to my soul, Soul, thou hast much goods laid up for many years; take thine ease, eat drink, and be merry.*

This man thought only of himself. Notice in his language that he spoke only of himself. He lived in a big world filled with great blessings. However, his own personal world was tiny, so tiny that it held only one person in it–himself. This rich man succeeded, but his success was failure. How many people have been blessed with things but have allowed those things to take them from God?

I remember the first time I heard about anyone in the real estate business showing a house on the Lord's Day. I remember how I felt about it. I heard about it over twenty-five years ago when I was preaching in a revival meeting in Georgia. A man who was in that church was a real estate agent. He could not wait for the Sunday service to be over so that he could show a house. I said, "Show a house on Sunday?" But this fellow replied, "It is the only time certain people can see it." Because of the relationship I had with that church, I was able to ask months later about that particular person. I found out that one Sunday became many Sundays, and Sunday afternoon work became Sunday morning and Sunday evening work also. There was an explosion of purchasing houses in that area; business was booming. People were talking about it being the fastest growing area in all of America. That real estate agent succeeded, but he failed. One cannot climb the ladder of success and leave God out!

The Parables of Jesus

Some of you look for blessings and possessions. What do you do with the things you have now? Why should God allow a man to make a thousand dollars a week if he will not tithe ten dollars out of a hundred dollars a week he makes now? Why should God bless someone with much when he will not give Him what belongs to Him now? One does not have to be wealthy to have the wrong attitude about possessions. We can have a selfish, sinful attitude just trying to make ends meet. Until we settle the matter of possessions, we will never settle the matter of God's blessing on our lives.

This fellow came to Christ and said that he had an inheritance; he wanted his inheritance. There is nothing wrong with his receiving the inheritance. It is obvious from what the Lord said that there was something wrong with his attitude toward his inheritance. This is the matter in which we need to ask God to help us examine our own hearts.

Let us remain dependent upon our heavenly Father all the days that we live. We must remember the failure of success. Our greatest failures are those things we consider to be success but are outside of God's will for our lives.

THE FUTURE OF SINNERS

In Luke 12:20 the Bible says, *"But God said unto him, Thou fool, this night thy soul shall be required of thee: then whose shall those things be, which thou hast provided?"* He neglected his soul. He lived and died as a fool, without God. His present was grand and glorious, but his future was *"the blackness of darkness for ever"* (Jude 13). I hope that when things like that are read or heard, no one ever rejoices over anyone going to hell.

The forty-one-year-old granddaughter of Ernest Hemingway was found dead in her tiny apartment. No one knows exactly what caused her death. There are suspicions that it was suicide, or perhaps some severe epileptic seizure. But in the report of her death, it was said

that Ms. Hemingway had tried to find something spiritual for the last few years of her life. She took trips to the Midwest and talked to native Indians. She went to India to talk to gurus. She was searching for something. The last recorded message she made was a message on an answering machine to her girlfriend whom she called shortly before her death. She said to her girlfriend, "God loves you. God loves you. And I love you."

Perhaps Ms. Hemingway knew the Lord Jesus as her Savior; I hope so. But if she did not, she was another hungry soul who searched for meaning and never found it. On one photo session twenty years before her death, she earned one million dollars from a magazine; it was not a pornographic magazine. She had multi-thousand dollar make-up contracts. Yet she battled alcoholism and all kinds of horrible things in her life. She searched for something. How sad that many are in this condition without Christ.

One cannot climb the ladder of success and leave God out!

We know the answer. While we watch people live and die all around us, we need to think of their future without Christ. We need to think about where they are headed. We need to think about their *"then;"* not just ours, but their *"then."* Let God use this to speak to our hearts about giving a clear gospel witness to people. We must give earnest attention to this one thing.

My wife and I stood at the hospital with one of my loved ones and talked and prayed with him before he went into surgery. He knew how serious it was. He said, "If I don't meet you here, I'll meet you in heaven." He wanted to live. When my mother went to see him in intensive care, he would ask her just like a child, "Do you think I am going to live?" I would go into the room and tell him, "You are going to live; Pop, you are going to live." The doctor gave us a good report; the heart procedure had gone well. There were a few little problems, but they would be straightened out, and he would live. Most people want to live, but we all are going into eternity–with God or without God!

THE FAITH OF THE SAVED

The Lord continued in Luke 12:21, *"So is he that layeth up treasure for himself, and is not rich toward God."* Notice that expression, *"rich toward God."* Then ask yourself, "Am I rich toward God?"

God's Word says in Luke 12:22-28,

> *And he said unto his disciples, Therefore, I say unto you, Take no thought for your life, what ye shall eat; neither for the body, what ye shall put on. The life is more than meat, and the body is more than raiment. Consider the ravens: for they neither sow nor reap; which neither have storehouse nor barn; and God feedeth them: how much more are ye better than the fowls? And which of you with taking thought can add to his stature one cubit? If ye then be not able to do that thing which is least, why take ye thought for the rest? Consider the lilies how they grow: they toil not, they spin not; and yet I say unto you, that Solomon in all his glory was not arrayed like one of these. If then God so clothe the grass, which is to day in the field, and tomorrow is cast into the oven; how much more will he clothe you, O ye of little faith?*

Think about what He is doing. Christ is emphasizing to His followers, "Don't let the world get you. Don't let the desire for things capture you. Don't put your roots down so deeply here. Not only is it wrong and sinful to live that way, but you will miss what God has for you." One can read this passage and notice the passion of Christ pressing the matter. The Bible says that Christ spoke *"unto his disciples."*

The Rich Fool

One man spoke up. Christ then spoke a parable to them. After the parable, He turned to His disciples and pressed this matter to them. Christ continued, *"And seek not ye what ye shall eat, or what ye shall drink, neither be ye of doubtful mind."*

The Bible says in Luke 12:30-34,

> *For all these things do the nations of the world seek after: and your Father knoweth that ye have need of these things. But rather seek ye the kingdom of God; and all these things shall be added unto you. Fear not, little flock; for it is your Father's good pleasure to give you the kingdom. Sell that ye have, and give alms; provide yourselves bags which wax not old, a treasure in the heavens that faileth not, where no thief approacheth, neither moth corrupteth. For where your treasure is, there will your heart be also.*

Christ is talking about the faith of the saved. The Lord Jesus is saying, "Live knowing your home is heaven. Live knowing who the Son of God really is. His Word is true. That is the way we should live our lives."

I cannot be around my family without thinking about how quickly time flies. Think of when your children were born; how quickly they have grown. Have we laid up treasures in heaven? So many people are living to leave something to this world; in doing so, they have invested so little in the world to come. Are you rich toward God?

A man who was a member of a certain church that operated a Christian college told me, "I served in that church and in that college for so many years, and not one time did a member in that church die and leave anything to that church or college." I was shocked to hear this. I am not necessarily saying this to encourage you to leave money to the church, though it would be a good idea to make sure the church is in your will. What I am saying to you is that we should consider our attitude toward the things of God. Our faith must rest in the Lord.

Consider this passage in the book of I Timothy. The Bible says in I Timothy 6:17, *"Charge them that are rich in this world, that they be not highminded, nor trust in uncertain riches, but in the living God, who giveth us richly all things to enjoy."* God gives all things, but why does He give us all things? He gives us these things to enjoy. Are you enjoying your life? There are many times I am not. Am I going to be the only person who is honest? Our greatest joy is in what God gives us; the faith life.

Our greatest failures are those things we consider to be success but are outside of God's will for our lives.

Not long before he died, Dr. Curtis Hutson preached one of his greatest sermons. He preached on the difference between sailing and rowing. He used the analogy of allowing the Spirit of God to get in our sail, taking us where He leads, or rowing and rowing in our own strength. Dr. Hutson said, "I have rowed nearly all of my life. Nearly all of my life I have tried to make it happen." He said, "I want to spend the rest of it sailing." Are you rowing or sailing? Our God meant for us to enjoy life in Him.

I Timothy 6:18-19 says, *"That they do good, that they be rich in good works, ready to distribute, willing to communicate; laying up in store for themselves a good foundation against the time to come, that they may lay hold on eternal life."* This does not mean we are doing things to have eternal life; it means that we understand what eternal life is all about.

Notice what God's Word says in James 2:5, *"Hearken, my beloved brethren, Hath not God chosen the poor of this world rich in faith, and heirs of the kingdom which he hath promised to them that love him?"* Are you rich in faith? If you are rich in other things, that is fine. I am glad God has blessed you and I am glad you honor the Lord. As you honor the Lord, I believe God will bless you even more. We can expect God to open the windows of heaven if we are willing to do what God has said. But are we rich in faith? This is what I want. I want you to be rich in faith. Covetous people who are materialistically minded cannot be rich in faith, and they cannot be happy in the Lord Jesus.

The Bible says in II Corinthians 5:1, *"For we know that if our earthly house of this tabernacle were dissolved, we have a building of God, an house not made with hands, eternal in the heavens."* Do you know that you have that building? I want to ask you this, what do you have up there? The reason we do not have much up there is that we do not trust Him much down here. When we start trusting Christ more down here, we will be putting more up there.

We say we love the Lord, but are we giving so that others will hear the gospel? Are we supporting missionaries around the world? Are we honoring God with the tithe? Do we take advantage of opportunities God gives us to help? Have we gotten to the place where we have had some measure of success and neglected God because of it? Think about this one thing–*"then."* Life on earth will soon be ended. *"Then whose shall those things be, which thou hast provided?"* May the Lord help us to live the Christian life our God has designed, faithfully in obedience to Him.

"And he answering said unto him, Lord, let it alone this year also, till I shall dig about it, and dung it: and if it bear fruit, well: and if not, then after that thou shalt cut it down."

Luke 13:8-9

BEARING FRUIT

ou have been placed on this earth for a special purpose. God said to the first man, Adam, *"Be fruitful and multiply."* Fruit bearing gives evidence of something much deeper. Not bearing fruit, or having a barren fruit tree gives evidence of something much deeper also. In other words, there is something that produces the fruit, and the lack of it causes the barrenness.

The Word of God says in Luke 13:6-9,

> *He spake also this parable; A certain man had a fig tree planted in his vineyard; and he came and sought fruit thereon, and found none. Then said he unto the dresser of his vineyard, Behold, these three years I come seeking fruit on this fig tree, and find none: cut it down; why cumbereth it the ground? And he answering said unto him, Lord, let*

> *it alone this year also, till I shall dig about it, and dung it: and if it bear fruit, well: and if not, then after that thou shalt cut it down."*

What does this parable mean? Parables are stories that Jesus Christ "placed alongside." The Lord gives us a story. Alongside that story, He points out something we need to know about the work of God–the way He gets things done, what He expects, and what He intends to do.

THE PRIVILEGE OF FRUIT BEARING

What does it mean to be right with God? Many people overemphasize results. They overemphasize the "fruit." The emphasis needs to be placed where God places the emphasis–being right with Him. When considering the fruit, more importantly, we must consider what produces the fruit.

In the Old Testament, in the fifth chapter of the book of Isaiah, the Lord speaks of His vineyard. God gave a distinct privilege to Israel. They are His special people, even though they have been set aside for this time. To them and through them, it is God's desire to make Himself known to the whole world. We understand from Scripture that the fig tree in the vineyard represents the nation of Israel. The vineyard is the special privileged place that God gave to His people Israel. In that special place, God placed His special people–His fig tree.

The Bible says in Isaiah 5:1-7,

> *Now will I sing to my wellbeloved a song of my beloved touching his vineyard. My wellbeloved hath a vineyard in a very fruitful hill: and he fenced it, and gathered out the stones thereof, and planted it with the choicest vine, and built a tower in the midst of it, and also made a winepress therein: and he looked*

that it should bring forth grapes, and it brought forth wild grapes. And now, O inhabitants of Jerusalem, and men of Judah, judge, I pray you, betwixt me and my vineyard. What could have been done more to my vineyard, that I have not done in it? wherefore, when I looked that it should bring forth grapes, brought it forth wild grapes? And now go to; I will tell you what I will do to my vineyard: I will take away the hedge thereof, and it shall be eaten up; and break down the wall thereof, and it shall be trodden down: and I will lay it waste: it shall not be pruned, nor digged; but there shall come up briers and thorns: I will also command the clouds that they rain no rain upon it. For the vineyard of the LORD of hosts is the house of Israel, and the men of Judah his pleasant plant: and he looked for judgment, but behold oppression; for righteousness, but behold a cry.

God said, "What could have been done more to My vineyard, that I have not done in it?" Contemplate that question. "Is there any more I could have done for you than I have already done? Could I have given you greater privilege? Could I have provided for you more than I have provided for you? Could there be anyone on the face of the earth to ever say that God has been better to him than I have been to you?" The answer is no.

God is saying, "I expect a certain thing from you; when I went to get that certain thing from you, I did not find it. I took tender care to build a fence around you, to build a tower to look out for you, to prune you, to make sure you were doing everything possible to be fruitful. Now, Israel, I am going to remove all the tender love and care that I gave and all the special attention I poured into you." God has not forgotten His people, Israel. He is not finished with the Jew. But for this time, they are set aside.

The Parables of Jesus

In interpretation, one must not see anything else other than the Jew; however, in application, one can see all of our lives. The principle remains true, not only for Israel, but for nations, churches, families, and individuals–for all of us. God is good to us. God has blessed us beyond measure. He has every right to expect that we be fruitful.

Notice what our Lord says in the closing part of Luke chapter twelve beginning with verse forty-nine and ending with verse fifty-three,

> *I am come to send fire on the earth; and what will I, if it be already kindled? But I have a baptism to be baptized with; and how am I straitened till it be accomplished! Suppose ye that I am come to give peace on earth? I tell you, Nay; but rather division: for from henceforth there shall be five in one house divided, three against two, and two against three. The father shall be divided against the son, and the son against the father; the mother against the daughter, and the daughter against the mother; the mother-in-law against her daughter-in-law, and the daughter-in-law against her mother-in-law.*

Who is the Great Divider? The Lord Jesus Christ is the Great Divider. When God saved you, Christ became the Great Divider in your life and family. Things we once loved to do, He divided from us. People that we once fellowshipped with, had things in common with, and even some of our own household, He divided us from. When we decided to live a life of righteousness for Jesus Christ, He became the Great Divider.

The Bible goes on to say in Luke 12:54, *"And he said also to the people, When ye see a cloud rise out of the west, straightway ye say, There cometh a shower; and so it is."* To the west was the Mediterranean Sea. When the clouds came from the sea onto the

land, it was known that those clouds brought water in them and that rain would come.

In Luke 12:55 the Bible says, *"And when ye see the south wind blow, ye say, There will be heat; and it cometh to pass."* To the south was the barren desert. As the winds crossed the desert, hot scorching winds would come upon them, and there would be heat. Everyone living in that area knew there would be heat if the winds blew across the south desert.

The Lord says in Luke 12:56-59,

> *Ye hypocrites, ye can discern the face of the sky and of the earth; but how is it that ye do not discern this time? Yea, and why even of yourselves judge ye not what is right? When thou goest with thine adversary to the magistrate, as thou are in the way, give diligence that thou mayest be delivered from him; lest he hale thee to the judge, and the judge deliver thee to the officer, and the officer cast thee into prison. I tell thee, thou shalt not depart thence, till thou hast paid the very last mite.*

Christ declared, "I want you to know that you are not going to escape." They were angry. They lashed out at Him. They felt that He had spoken against them and against their sin. What happens when we are convicted of our sins? Are we willing to repent and to change the way we are living? Are we willing to say, "Lord, you are right and I am wrong." This is our time of opportunity to serve the Lord Jesus.

The Parables of Jesus

THE PERSONAL ACCOUNTABILITY OF FRUIT BEARING

Notice the reason that Christ gave this parable. The Bible says in Luke 13:1, *"There were present at that season some that told him of the Galileans, whose blood Pilate had mingled with their sacrifices."* The people blurted out saying, "You think that we are so bad, but what about those Galileans? These Galileans, in the act of sacrificing, were killed by Pilate. They must have been terrible." The people believed that any type of calamity that came to one's life was because of sin. They believed that because these people had a terrible thing happen to them, it had to be because they were such terrible sinners. These Jews in Judea were especially delighted to call attention to the Galileans who had been killed.

> *When we decided to live a life of righteousness for Jesus Christ, He became the Great Divider.*

The people who were talking to the Lord were actually saying, "Wait a minute. Let us compare ourselves to the Galileans that Pilate killed. They were much worse than we are." We are never going to be right with God as long as we compare ourselves with others. If you want to go through life trying to find someone doing less than you are, you can do it. But you can never be right with God by comparing yourself with other people.

The Lord said in verses two and three of Luke chapter thirteen, *"And Jesus answering said unto them, Suppose ye that these Galileans were sinners above all the Galileans, because they suffered such things? I tell you, Nay: but, except ye repent, ye shall all likewise perish."* Think of that. Christ changed the whole perspective. He told the people, "We are not going to talk about those Galileans;

we are going to talk about you." He said, *"Except ye repent, ye shall all likewise perish."*

In Luke 13:4 Christ said, *"Or those eighteen, upon whom the tower in Siloam fell, and slew them, think ye that they were sinners above all men that dwelt in Jerusalem?"* Evidently, when the tower of Siloam fell and eighteen people were killed, everyone knew about it. Christ was saying to them, "Are you saying that you think the eighteen that died at Siloam were the greatest sinners in Jerusalem just because they were there when the tower fell? Are you saying that the tower fell on them because God was punishing them for their great crime against Him? Is that the way you have it all figured out?"

We are never going to be right with God as long as we compare ourselves with others.

Christ answers His own question, *"I tell you, Nay: but, except ye repent, ye shall all likewise perish."* In this short parable of just a few verses, Christ is talking to us about how to be right with God. It is not about someone else's privilege, but our privilege. It is not about someone else's accountability, but our accountability.

Christ tells a story about a vineyard, but in the vineyard there was a fig tree. That was not unusual. On certain parts or parcels of ground in a vineyard, other types of plants could be planted. Certain plants, in accordance with God's Law in the Bible, including the fig tree, could be planted in a vineyard.

In the vineyard, which represents the sacred place that God selected for the Jew, God planted His people. They are represented by the fig tree. He put them there to be fruitful. He came seeking fruit and found none. Note again in Luke 13:6-9,

> *He spake also this parable; A certain man had a fig tree planted in his vineyard; and he came and sought*

> *fruit thereon, and found none. Then said he unto the dresser of his vineyard, Behold, these three years I come seeking fruit on this fig tree, and find none: cut it down; why cumbereth it the ground? And he answering said unto him, Lord, let it alone this year also, till I shall dig about it, and dung it: and if it bear fruit, well: and if not, then after that thou shalt cut it down.*

The Bible says in verse six, *"A certain man had a fig tree planted in his vineyard; and he came and sought fruit thereon, and found none."* He had every right to come and seek fruit because he expected it to bear fruit. It was supposed to bear fruit.

Verse seven says, *"Then said he unto the dresser of his vineyard, Behold, these three years I come seeking fruit on this fig tree, and find none."* He said, "I've been coming for three years seeking fruit on this tree. No fruit!" Then he said, "Cut it down." This is a solemn thought.

No wonder some churches and some Christians are having such trouble. They have God's judgment on them because there is no fruit. They are doing nothing. They are just taking up space. They are doing absolutely nothing to reproduce.

He said, "Cut it down!" From God's declaration of cutting it down, notice what He said, *"Why cumbereth it the ground?"* When a fruit tree does not produce fruit, it is taking ground that could be given to some other fruit-bearing plant. So quite naturally, the ground that was used by the tree was nothing more than wasted space.

I believe that there was a note of tenderness in his voice when the dresser of the vineyard said in verse eight, *"Lord, let it alone this year also, till I shall dig about it, and dung it."* In other words, "I'm going to disturb the ground around the tree. Then I'm going to add nourishment to the ground. I'm going to dig around it and dung it to fertilize it. Let me do that, would you please?"

Then the Bible says in verse nine, *"And if it bear fruit, well: and if not, then after that thou shalt cut it down."* In other words, "Give me an opportunity to work, disturbing the ground and adding nourishment." This is a time of mercy. It is a time for digging and dunging. It is a time for things to be disturbed. The Lord is at work.

I believe we are living between God saying, *"Cut it down,"* and His coming again. He is digging and dunging. He is disturbing our soul. Many nations, many churches, many families, and many individuals have had this opportunity. What more could be done to disturb our ground?

After God has disturbed the soil and poured in what we need for nourishment to produce fruit, He has every right to look again and expect that we are bearing fruit. After no fruit, no fruit, no fruit, what if the Lord says, "Cut it down"? Do you believe as I believe that we are living on God's mercy?

> *When the holiness of God demands, the mercy of God answers, "I will pay the price."*

May God awaken us that we should be doing more than just taking space on the earth. *"Why cumbereth it the ground?"* Why is it just taking up space if it is not going to produce fruit? God gave us this time, this place, this space, so that we might produce fruit and honor Him.

Think of how many people go to our churches, read the Bible, listen to the Word of God, and get the nourishment poured upon them, but never produce any fruit. Then they go through divine disturbances where God digs, but no change. I think that at any moment He might pass through again and say, "Cut it down!"

"Why cumbereth it the ground?" Why is it there? It is there so it can reproduce and bear fruit. Christians are to reproduce other

The Parables of Jesus

Christians. Churches are to bear other churches. We are to live our lives honoring God, exemplifying Christ.

What we find here is an example of the way God works. God tells us that this is sin; but He gives a time to repent. When the holiness of God demands, the mercy of God answers, "I will pay the price." A holy God said that men must die for their sin and go to hell forever trying to pay for their sins. God's Son, the Lord Jesus, said, "I'll die for them. I'll pay the sin debt."

How do we get right with God? It involves seeing our own accountability to the Lord. Our eyes are on everyone else and everything else. The only race we ever have to run is the race against the opportunity and ability God has given us. If we are ever to be right with God, we must say, "Lord, I will stand alone before You and I will answer to You for my ability, privilege, and opportunity." This is the way to be right with God. God brings us into the place where we see ourselves personally accountable to the Lord.

In interpretation, this parable is about the nation of Israel; but in application, it is about all we should be as a church, all we should be as a blessed nation, all we should be in our Christian homes, and all we should be as individuals. God has done so much for us. He has blessed us. He said, *"If it bear fruit."* There is evidence of the right kind of life when fruit is borne. I want to be a fruit-bearing Christian. The Lord has every right to expect me to be a fruit-bearing Christian. I have life in me; not my life, but His life in me. I am partaker of the divine nature. The Lord lives in me.

If there is no fruit in your life, one of two things is evident. Either you are not abiding in the Lord, or you have never been born again. As Christians, we are all to bear fruit. We place the emphasis sometimes on the fruit; let us place the emphasis first on the root. If we are right, we will bear fruit.

In too many places, we have equated activity with spirituality. Too many times we have talked to people and given them the idea that if they simply do more, they are going to be more of what they should be. I do not have to convince you that I think we should be busy for the Lord. I do not have to convince you that I believe in the urgency of the hour. I do not have to convince you that we are living with the fact of the imminent return of Jesus Christ. I want to love His appearing.

Let us turn our attention to II Peter chapter one. One of the ways we understand Scripture is by comparing Scripture with Scripture. I appreciate every good thing we can read that God has given other authors to pen in books that we can buy, borrow, and read, but the greatest commentary on the Bible is the Bible.

The Bible says in II Peter 1:1-5,

> *Simon Peter, a servant and an apostle of Jesus Christ, to them that have obtained like precious faith with us through the righteousness of God and our Savior Jesus Christ: grace and peace be multiplied unto you though the knowledge of God, and of Jesus our Lord, according as his divine power hath given unto us all things that pertain unto life and godliness, through the knowledge of him that hath called us to glory and virtue: whereby are given unto us exceeding great and precious promises: that by these ye might be partakers of the divine nature, having escaped the corruption that is in the world through lust. And beside this, giving all diligence, add to your faith...*

The only race we ever have to run is the race against the opportunity and ability God has given us.

Notice the language here, *"Add to your faith."* The Bible does not say add faith; it says add *to* your faith. Some people have the idea that if a person finally gets enough information about Christ, he is a Christian. No! Salvation is immediate. Just as physical life begins with conception, salvation is also instantaneous. Once there is conception, that human being is going to live forever as long as God lives. Once there is regeneration, we are born into God's family. The moment we "faith" the finished work of Jesus Christ, the Lord comes to live in us. We live forever as children of God, with God. We are born into God's family.

Once we have faith, we should add to our faith. God says in II Peter 1:5, *"Add to your faith virtue..."* Virtue has to do with character. Character has to do with what we are, not what we do. We may live virtuously; but if we live virtuously, it is because we have virtue. We may "do" right things; but the emphasis is on "being" right, so we will do right things. We may bear fruit; but if we bear fruit, it is because we are right with God.

Let us continue with II Peter 1:5-9,

> *...and to virtue knowledge; and to knowledge temperance; and to temperance patience; and to patience godliness; and to godliness brotherly kindness and to brotherly kindness charity. For if these things be in you, and abound, they make you that ye shall neither be barren nor unfruitful in the knowledge of our Lord Jesus Christ. But he that lacketh these things is blind, and cannot see afar off and hath forgotten that he was purged from his old sins.*

In this passage, the Lord is talking to Christians. He says that they have not been living as Christians. God tells us in II Peter 1:9-10 what we need to do if we are going to be fruitful.

> *But he that lacketh these things is blind, and cannot see afar off, and hath forgotten that he was purged from his old sins. Wherefore the rather, brethren, give diligence to make your calling and election sure: for if ye do these things, ye shall never fall.*

We should bear fruit. Someone once said that the fruit of a Christian is another Christian. This is true. But there is also the fruit of the Spirit.

In Galatians 5:22 the Bible says, *"But the fruit of the Spirit is love, joy, peace, long-suffering, gentleness, goodness, faith, meekness, temperance: against such there is no law."* The word *"fruit"* is singular.

This "fruit" is like a cluster of grapes. There are nine grapes on this individual, singular fruit. This "fruit" is produced in our lives by the Holy Spirit. In other words, the Holy Spirit produces love. The Holy Spirit produces joy. The Holy Spirit produces peace. The Holy Spirit produces longsuffering. The Holy Spirit produces gentleness. The Holy Spirit produces goodness. The Holy Spirit produces faith. The Holy Spirit produces meekness. The Holy Spirit produces temperance.

What is evident when this "fruit of the Spirit" is not in our lives? It is evident that we are not being the Christians we should be. We are not abiding in Him. We are not living obedient lives.

Do you desire to be this kind of fruit-bearing Christian? Remember, the parable is regarding Israel. The Lord is inspecting them, and there is no fruit. In application, we must bear fruit.

Let us look again in John chapter fifteen. The Bible says in John 15:1-5,

> *I am the true vine, and my Father is the husbandman. Every branch in me that beareth not fruit he taketh away: and every branch that beareth fruit, he purgeth it, that it may bring forth more fruit.*

> *Now ye are clean through the word which I have spoken unto you. Abide in me, and I in you. As the branch cannot bear fruit of itself, except it abide in the vine; no more can ye, except ye abide in me. I am the vine, ye are the branches: he that abideth in me, and I in him, the same bringeth forth much fruit: for without me ye can do nothing.*

The word *"fruit"* is found in verse two; *"more fruit"* is found at the conclusion of verse two; and in verse five is *"much fruit."* I want to be a *"much fruit"* Christian. Not simply *"fruit"* and *"more fruit,"* I want to be a *"much fruit"* Christian. John 15:6-7 tells us why.

> *If a man abide not in me, he is cast forth as a branch, and is withered; and men gather them, and cast them into the fire, and they are burned. If ye abide in me, and my words abide in you, ye shall ask what ye will, and it shall be done unto you.*

How do we bear fruit? By being right. How are we right with God? By abiding in Christ and recognizing our own individual accountability to God.

THE PURPOSE OF FRUIT BEARING

Our purpose in fruit bearing is to bring glory to the Lord. What is the parable about? The vineyard was the Lord's; the fig tree was the Lord's. The parable was about the Lord getting glory from His vineyard and His fig tree. He gave the vineyard; He gave the fig tree. It was all His.

What is it all about? It is not about applauding men. It is not about praising men. We should say, "Lord, I want to bear fruit." But why bear fruit? We should want to bear much fruit. Why bear much fruit?

Bearing Fruit

The Bible says in John 15:7-8, *"If ye abide in me, and my words abide in you, ye shall ask what ye will, and it shall be done unto you. Herein is my Father glorified, that ye bear much fruit; so shall ye be my disciples."* If we bear much fruit, God is glorified.

We must hunger and thirst after the Lord. The fruit is not the goal; glorifying the Lord is the goal. As long as we desire to glorify the Lord, the Lord will smile on us, bless us, and provide us with what we need. Let us ask God to help us to bear much fruit for His glory.

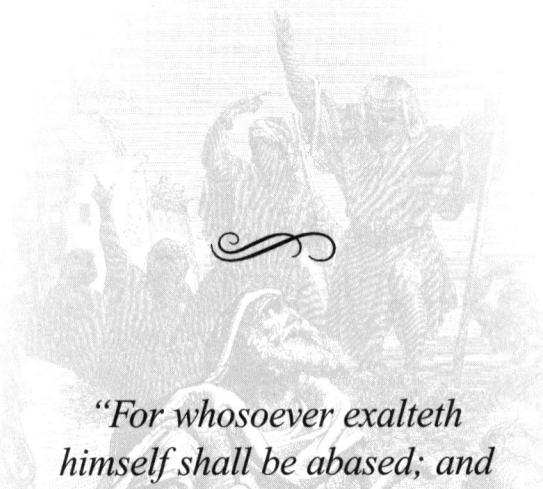

"For whosoever exalteth himself shall be abased; and he that humbleth himself shall be exalted."

Luke 14:11

Chapter Seven

Those Who Are Blessed

he Bible teaches that the Lord desires to bless us. It is my desire to be blessed of God, because as I am blessed, I can be a blessing to others and bring glory to the Lord. In Luke 14:1-15 we find the Lord Jesus giving a parable about those who are blessed. The Bible says,

> And it came to pass, as he went into the house of one of the chief Pharisees to eat bread on the sabbath day, that they watched him. And, behold, there was a certain man before him which had the dropsy. And Jesus answering spake unto the lawyers and Pharisees, saying, Is it lawful to heal on the sabbath day? And they held their peace. And he took him, and healed him, and let him go; and answered them, saying, Which of you shall have an ass or an ox fallen into a pit, and will not straightway pull him out on the sabbath day? And they could not answer him again to

> these things. And he put forth a parable to those which were bidden, when he marked how they chose out the chief rooms; saying unto them, When thou art bidden of any man to a wedding, sit not down in the highest room; lest a more honorable man than thou be bidden of him; and he that bade thee and him come and say to thee, Give this man place; and thou begin with shame to take the lowest room. But when thou art bidden, go and sit down in the lowest room; that when he that bade thee cometh, he may say unto thee, Friend, go up higher: then shalt thou have worship in the presence of them that sit at meat with thee. For whosoever exalteth himself shall be abased; and he that humbleth himself shall be exalted. Then said he also to him that bade him, When thou makest a dinner or a supper, call not thy friends, nor thy brethren, neither thy kinsmen, nor thy rich neighbors; lest they also bid thee again, and a recompense be made thee. But when thou makest a feast, call the poor, the maimed, the lame, the blind: and thou shalt be blessed; for they cannot recompense thee: for thou shalt be recompensed at the resurrection of the just. And when one of them that sat at meat with him heard these things, he said unto him, Blessed is he that shall eat bread in the kingdom of God.

The Bible says in Luke 14:11, *"For whosoever exalteth himself shall be abased; and he that humbleth himself shall be exalted."* This particular parable is about humility. If one declares that he has humility, then at that moment he does not have it. Christ spoke plainly, *"For whosoever exalteth himself shall be abased; and he that humbleth himself shall be exalted."*

Consider what the Bible says in I Peter 5:5-6,

> *Likewise, ye younger, submit yourselves unto the elder. Yea, all of you be subject one to another, and be*

clothed with humility: for God resisteth the proud, and giveth grace to the humble. Humble yourselves therefore under the mighty hand of God, that he may exalt you in due time.

Note the expression, *"subject one to another."* The parable in Luke chapter fourteen is dealing with this. It is not our business to take over and make ourselves the boss. *"Be subject one to another."* Do you have a spirit of submission?

CHRIST PREACHED

We have a calling to humility. Let us go back to the teaching that Christ gave. Notice Christ's preaching. The Bible says in Luke 14:1, *"And it came to pass, as he went into the house of one of the chief Pharisees."* Some places are harder to preach in than other places. I think that this was a hard place in which to preach. Christ is in the house of one of the chief Pharisees. The Bible says that as the Lord Jesus went in *"to eat bread on the sabbath day, that they watched him. And, behold, there was a certain man before him which had the dropsy."*

They brought a sick man to Him, not because they cared for the sick man, but because they wanted to see if the Lord Jesus would heal him on the Sabbath. The Lord knew what they were thinking. This reminds me that not everyone comes to church for the same reason. Some come to church and find fault when they arrive. Here, the Lord was in the house of a chief Pharisee on the Sabbath day, and the Pharisees brought in a very sick man. They were watching; He knew they were watching. They thought it was all right for them to have a party and a feast on the Sabbath, but they thought it was wrong to heal the sick on the Sabbath.

Christ asked a question, *"Is it lawful to heal on the sabbath day? And they held their peace. And he took him, and healed him, and let him go."* We read of this account in just a few words, but think what went on there in that house. The lawyers and Pharisees were all watching. They were spying on Him. They had a sick man in the room, a man they did not even want there. He was an annoyance to them; he did not fit in that crowd. They brought him because they wanted to see if the Lord would heal him on the Sabbath day. The Lord Jesus asked them, *"Is it lawful to heal on the sabbath day?"* They would not answer Him. He healed the man and let him go.

We serve a courageous Savior who preached courageously; He spoke the truth with piercing conviction.

The Bible continues in verse five, *"And answered them, saying, Which of you shall have an ass or an ox fallen into a pit, and will not straightway pull him out on the sabbath day? And they could not answer him again to these things."*

Christ asked them a question. He asked them to imagine that they had an ox that they cared for, or a beast of burden that they cared for, and it fell into trouble on the Sabbath day. What would they do? They would not answer. The Lord Jesus was saying to the lawyers and Pharisees, "I love this man who needed healing. You do not care. You would rather catch Me than see the healing of the man because you do not care about him."

By this time, the crowd was growing hostile. It is one thing to preach against sin; it is another thing to preach against sin right where you find it. Preaching against sin is hard; preaching against sin right where one finds it, in the face of it, when one uncovers it, is even more difficult. Christ first preached against the actions of those who stood in His face. He then preached against the one who asked Him to come. Christ said in Luke 14:7-9,

> *And he put forth a parable to those which were bidden, when he marked how they chose out the chief rooms; saying unto them, When thou art bidden of any man to a wedding, sit not down in the highest*

Those Who Are Blessed

> *room; lest a more honourable man than thou be bidden of him; and he that bade thee and him come and say to thee, Give this man place; and thou begin with shame to take the lowest room.*

At a feast, according to what is known about eastern culture at the time of Christ, there were certain ways of setting tables and the seats at those tables. Most often, the tables were in threes. Among each of those three settings, there was a chief seat where the most honored person was to sit. Whoever was in that seat was the most honored person.

The Lord was in the house of one of the chief Pharisees. Well-to-do guests were invited to the feast, along with the sick man, to see what Christ would do. As these guests came in, they ran to the chief seats. They were all fighting for the best seats and the seat of honor. They wanted to be the person who was to be the most honored, the most respected, the most exalted. The chair was almost like a throne. The person who sat there received all the adoration. That was the first place these guests went. Christ marked it by saying,

> *When thou art bidden of any man to a wedding, sit not down in the highest room; lest a more honourable man than thou be bidden of him; and he that bade thee and him come and say to thee, Give this man place, and thou begin with shame to take the lowest room.*

He told them that they had done exactly the opposite of what they should have done. He told them that they had bad manners because their motives were bad. Can you imagine going to a party and telling everyone who comes, "You have bad manners; the reason you have bad manners is that you have bad motives; you have bad motives because you have a bad heart"?

We serve a courageous Savior who preached courageously; He spoke the truth with piercing conviction. Christ reprimanded the people, "So you come and take the highest seat, and a person who is supposed to receive that kind of honor comes in, and you are asked to get out of his seat. You leave his seat in shame, with head bowed low and take the lowest seat where you should have gone to begin with."

Let us continue. The Bible says in Luke 14:10-11,

> *But when thou art bidden, go and sit down in the lowest room; that when he that bade thee cometh, he may say unto thee, Friend, go up higher: then shalt thou have worship in the presence of them that sit at meat with thee. For whosoever exalteth himself shall be abased; and he that humbleth himself shall be exalted.*

This is so plain. How many of us are so busy looking out for ourselves and for our own good? Is it good for us? Is it best for me? Is it advantageous for me? Is this my best opportunity? Will this work out in a way that puts me on top? Someone may say, "Shouldn't we try to do our best?" This is not what we are talking about. We are talking about leaving God out entirely. We try to work our way up, push our way, force our way by making decisions on the basis of what it will do or not do for us. There is a God in heaven who takes care of His own children. He can be trusted to take care of us.

It is one thing to preach against sin; it is another thing to preach against sin right where you find it.

Christ is preaching here. His preaching brings us right to the very heart of what we do and who we are. The Spirit of God shines the light on us and says, "Look and you will see who you are by what you do, how you are always looking out for yourself, how you are trying to take the chief place to be exalted. You are revealing what is in your heart; not just about how you are going to treat people, but how you think about God and what God can do for you or not do for you." If I am consistently living by force and exalting myself, I am declaring with every action that I do not have faith to trust God to take care of me.

CHRIST PRACTICED WHAT HE PREACHED

People do not mind listening to someone if they believe that he "practices what he preaches." Lining up with the Bible is a goal that we are trying to achieve. God forbid that any of us get the idea that we are perfect, but our Lord is perfect. He practiced what He preached. He preached about humility and He practiced humility. The Bible says in Philippians 2:1-3,

> *If there be therefore any consolation in Christ, if any comfort of love, if any fellowship of the Spirit, if any bowels and mercies, fulfill ye my joy, that ye be likeminded, having the same love, being of one accord, of one mind. Let nothing be done through strife or vainglory; but in lowliness of mind let each esteem other better than themselves.*

How often do we find ourselves doing exactly the opposite? The Word of God says in Romans 12:10, *"In honour preferring one another."* We cannot wait until we get to the front of the line; we push and shove our way through life. We demonstrate bad manners because we have bad motives. We say there is a God, but we live as if there is no God to take care of us. There is a God who takes care of those who trust Him. Christ did not simply preach this, He practiced it.

The Bible says in Philippians 2:4, *"Look not every man on his own things, but every man also on the things of others."* What a different kind of church, what a different kind of home, what a different kind of family life Christian people would have if they practiced this. How different the workplace would be if Christian people practiced this. It would be like pouring holy oil on all the friction we have in life. People would not create a fuss about where they sit or who gets their seat. People would not complain about petty things; they would be helping, ministering, and serving. You may ask, "Does anyone live such a life?" Christ did.

The Parables of Jesus

The Bible says in Philippians 2:5-8,

> *Let this mind be in you, which was also in Christ Jesus: who, being in the form of God, thought it not robbery to be equal with God: but made himself of no reputation, and took upon him the form of a servant, and was made in the likeness of men: and being found in fashion as a man, he humbled himself, and became obedient unto death, even the death of the cross.*

What did that get Him? It got Him the greatest honor and the greatest glory this world will ever know. Philippians 2:9-11 says,

> *Wherefore God also hath highly exalted him, and given him a name which is above every name: that at the name of Jesus every knee should bow, of things in heaven, and things in earth, and things under the earth; and that every tongue should confess that Jesus Christ is Lord, to the glory of God the Father.*

Christ practiced this humility. He humbled Himself. The greatest of all humbled Himself to the least. He became the least among us, because He bore the sin of us all. He bled and died for our sin. He not only preached, but He also practiced what He preached. Many of us hear the preaching. Our sin is not that we do not agree with it; our sin is that we do not live it.

Our Lord was in this ruler's house, this chief of the Pharisees; the guests all came in and rushed for the most prominent places, and He marked it. He marks when we rush to those prominent places, looking out for ourselves, exalting ourselves, making ourselves look good. He marks when we say the things that are self-promoting, self-gratifying, and self-exalting. Do you not know that Christ marks those things? He preached to them about their sin of self-exaltation. He had a right to say those things because He practiced humility.

Those Who Are Blessed

The Bible says in Luke 14:11, *"For whosoever exalteth himself shall be abased; and he that humbleth himself shall be exalted. Then said he also to him that bade him..."* In verse seven, He spoke to those that were bidden. Now He spoke singularly to the person who bade Him. He spoke to the guests, now He speaks to the host. What does He have to say to the host? He says in Luke 14:12-13,

> *When thou makest a dinner or a supper, call not thy friends, nor thy brethren, neither thy kinsmen, nor thy rich neighbours; lest they also bid thee again, and a recompence be made thee. But when thou makest a feast, call the poor, the maimed, the lame, the blind.*

If I am consistently living by force and exalting myself, I am declaring with every action that I do not have faith to trust God to take care of me.

Christ was saying to the Pharisee, "I'll tell you what you have done. You have invited everyone that you thought could do something for you. The only reason you have done what you have done is to try to get something from them by doing something for them. The next time you have supper, you should go out and find the poor, the lame, and the blind. Invite the people who can do nothing for you in return. There is a God in heaven who will see your action and your motive and reward you. Trust Him."

We do not live as the Lord has instructed us to live. We go through life hoping for a return. We get angry when we give people something and they do not say, "Thank you." They should thank you; but if you do what you are supposed to do, God will take care of the rest. Are we going to spend our lives thinking we have to get an equal return on what we invest in other people? Is that the way we are going to spend our lives, or are we going to let God take care of that? We must decide.

We wear our feelings on our shoulders and get them knocked off all the time. We say, "Nobody said a thing about what I have done. I thought they would have recognized me." Wait a minute. Why did you do what you did? Did you do it as unto the Lord? There is a world of difference between inviting the rich neighbors, the people who can do great things for you, or inviting the people who can never do anything in return for you. Think again of the Lord Jesus. We could never give back to Him what He has given to us. He gave Himself–the sinless Son of God. We love and adore Him, and we want to serve Him because we love and adore Him for what He has done for us.

CHRIST PROMISED TO BLESS

Christ said in Luke 14:14, *"And thou shalt be blessed; for they cannot recompense thee: for thou shalt be recompensed at the resurrection of the just."* They cannot bless you, but God will. This is a promise. Do you want to be blessed? If you really want to be blessed, then this is how–give your life away.

There is a story of two young missionary men who allowed God to capture their hearts, and they wanted to tell the lost about Christ. They heard about a slave owner who had three thousand slaves working for him, and he said that he would never allow anyone to preach the gospel or come with any message of salvation. The two young men that knew the Lord and loved the Lord found out about those slaves. In order to get the message of Christ to them, these men sold themselves as slaves to that slave owner; not for a while, but for the rest of their lives. The young men went in among those slaves to win them to Christ. Their families knew that they would never see them again. They were about to enter into slavery by living the remainder of their lives, witnessing to those slaves. Their loved ones wept as they said goodbye to them. One of them cried out as the men left those whom they loved, "May the Lamb that was slain receive the reward of His suffering." Let me tell you that their reward in heaven will be great.

Those Who Are Blessed

I feel so ashamed that so much of my life has been lived with the idea of doing with the hope of getting. We should all be ashamed. When we live that way, we are living as if there is no God. The Lord Jesus said, "I will bless you." This is His promise.

Someone was listening. In Luke 14:15 the Bible says, *"And when one of them that sat at meat with him heard these things, he said unto him, Blessed is he that shall eat bread in the kingdom of God."* That was not a remark of scoffing. It dawned on this listener that what Christ said was true. Like this listener, we need to recognize that what Christ said is still true today. Do you want God's blessing on your life? Do you want to be found among those who are truly blessed of God? I do. May God help us to live out this truth day by day.

*"So likewise, whosoever he
be of you that forsaketh not
all that he hath, he cannot
be my disciple."*

Luke 14:33

Discipleship

he Lord Jesus Christ has called us to follow Him. Is it your heart's desire to be a follower of the Lord Jesus Christ? In the Bible, He sets before us what we must do if we intend to truly follow Him. Not everyone who is identified with Christ is truly following Him.

The Bible says in Luke 14:25-15:2,

> *And there went great multitudes with him: and he turned, and said unto them, If any man come to me, and hate not his father, and mother, and wife, and children, and brethren, and sisters, yea, and his own life also, he cannot be my disciple. And whosoever doth not bear his cross, and come after me, cannot be my disciple. For which of you, intending to build a tower, sitteth not down first, and counteth the cost, whether he have sufficient to finish it? Lest haply,*

after he hath laid the foundation, and is not able to finish it, all that behold it begin to mock him, saying, This man began to build, and was not able to finish. Or what king, going to make war against another king, sitteth not down first, and consulteth whether he be able with ten thousand to meet him that cometh against him with twenty thousand? Or else, while the other is yet a great way off, he sendeth an ambassage, and desireth conditions of peace. So likewise, whosoever he be of you that forsaketh not all that he hath, he cannot be my disciple. Salt is good: but if the salt have lost his savour, wherewith shall it be seasoned? It is neither fit for the land, nor yet for the dunghill; but men cast it out. He that hath ears to hear, let him hear. Then drew near unto him all the publicans and sinners for to hear him. And the Pharisees and scribes murmured, saying, This man receiveth sinners, and eateth with them.

Three times in this passage our Lord repeats a phrase. In the twenty-sixth verse, the Bible says, *"He cannot be my disciple."* In the twenty-seventh verse the Bible says, *"Cannot be my disciple."* In the thirty-third verse the Bible says, *"He cannot be my disciple."*

Salvation is the gift of God. The Bible says in Ephesians 2:8-9, *"For by grace are ye saved through faith; and that not of yourselves: it is the gift of God: not of works, lest any man should boast."* When someone read John 3:16 and explained the gospel to me, I knew very little about the Lord; I knew little about His Word. A concerned Christian explained that Jesus Christ loved me and died for my sin, and that He was buried and rose from the dead. I understood that I was a sinner, and God was holy and perfect. He gave His Son for my sin. I asked the Lord to forgive my sin, and I received Him as my Savior. At that moment, I was born into God's family; I became a

child of God. I would have gone to heaven if I had died the next moment; not on my merit, but on His merit; not because of what I had done, but because of what He had done for me. I was just as saved that moment as I am this moment. Heaven is my home, I am sure of it; not because I deserve it, but because He paid the price for me to have it.

In this parable, we are dealing with discipleship. Many people are misled about discipleship. We try to disciple people once they trust Christ as Savior, trying to get them grounded in the Word of God. But to become a disciple means more than most make of it.

The Lord lays down the terms for discipleship. Consider John 8:29-31:

> *And he that sent me is with me: the Father hath not left me alone; for I do always those things that please him. As he spake these words, many believed on him. Then said Jesus to those Jews which believed on him, If ye continue in my word, then are ye my disciples indeed.*

Continuing in His Word was not a condition of becoming a Christian, but it gave evidence of discipleship. Some say that to be a disciple is to be a follower. It goes beyond being a follower to being like Christ. If you are going to be a disciple of the Lord Jesus Christ, a follower of the Lord Jesus Christ, you must live as He has told us to live.

THE MUST OF DISCIPLESHIP

When Christ says three times, *"He cannot be my disciple," "Cannot be my disciple," "He cannot be my disciple,"* we see what He says must be done in order to be His disciple. The Word of God says in Luke 14:25, *"And there went great multitudes with him."* Luke, under the inspiration of the Spirit of God, pens these words very descriptively. There was a huge group of people, multitudes, following the Lord. He turned and spoke to them. His audience was not just a handful of people, but a great crowd that was following Him. The Bible says that He said to them, *"If any man come to me, and hate not his father, and mother, and wife, and children, and brethren, and sisters, yea, and his own life also, he cannot be my disciple."*

> *If you are going to be a disciple of the Lord Jesus Christ, a follower of the Lord Jesus Christ, you must live as He has told us to live.*

The Lord turned and faced the multitudes and laid down these terms. Many who have heard this passage expounded upon have heard the idea that oriental languages use exaggerated contrasts. Instead of several degrees of emotion and commitment laid out before us, love and hate are contrasted. Do not miss the point by overemphasizing the difference between love and hate. I certainly do not hate my mother and I do not hate my father. I do not hate my wife or my children. I am sure that you have heard that our love for our families should look like hate compared to our love for Christ. What can we find on earth that is more noble and blessed of God and more precious than our relationships with our families? What is more precious than the love that we have and the command that we have to obey and honor? What is more precious than the love that we share in our married union? What is more precious than the love that God gives in our hearts for our children? What does He mean? I do not want to soften the meaning. Any time there comes a conflict between father and mother, husband and wife, son or daughter, or a conflict between any of these and Christ, Christ must be chosen.

Some men complain about their mate not being the spiritual person she ought to be. They have missed the mark entirely. Most of the time, it is not the woman who is not the spiritual person she should

be; it is the man who is not the spiritual person he should be. The wife will respond to someone who gives the Lord His rightful place.

Early on in marriage, every man must establish himself as the spiritual leader in his home. You may marry someone that is full of emotion or strong will; or you may marry a very compliant person. Do not think that marrying a very compliant person is going to naturally make you the head of the house, because those compliant people know how to wiggle their way around to get what they want.

When it comes to any family member, there has to be a decision in our hearts as to whether we are going to give in to them or follow Christ. This does not mean that we be neglectful of family and let our families go to the Devil to follow the Lord; it does not mean this at all. Some people have taken this passage as an excuse for not being the father or the husband they should be. It does not mean that you have to win the world and let your family go to hell. When there is a conflict or a decision to be made, when

Any time there comes a conflict between father and mother, husband and wife, son or daughter, or a conflict between any of these and Christ, Christ must be chosen.

there is a tug on your heart and you know clearly what Christ would desire you to do, you must choose Christ. If there is conflict about whether or not you can follow Him with your whole heart because of family, houses, lands, or whatever the case may be, you must follow Christ. If there is conflict between whether Christ is going to be the Lord in a matter or not, you must choose Christ.

The Bible says in Luke 14:27, *"And whosoever doth not bear his cross, and come after me, cannot be my disciple."* What does this mean, *"bear his cross"*? Bear not the cross of Christ, but your own cross. Some of us think that our cross is our own personal suffering. This is not true. Some people think that their cross is some sort of thorn they have to deal with in life. You may say, "I've got my cross. God gave me my cross to bear." You are feeling sorry for yourself.

In Philippians 2:1-8 the Bible says,

> *If there be therefore any consolation in Christ, if any comfort of love, if any fellowship of the Spirit, if any bowels and mercies, fulfill ye my joy, that ye be like-minded, having the same love, being of one accord, of one mind. Let nothing be done through strife or vainglory; but in lowliness of mind let each esteem other better than themselves. Look not every man on his own things, but every man also on the things of others. Let this mind be in you, which was also in Christ Jesus: who, being in the form of God, thought it not robbery to be equal with God: but made himself of no reputation, and took upon him the form of a servant, and was made in the likeness of men. And being found in fashion as a man, he humbled himself, and became obedient unto death, even the death of the cross.*

Christ emptied Himself for others. Our cross-bearing is not sickness or a physical problem. Cross-bearing is not someone or something that God puts in our path. If we identify the cross with Christ, we see that Christ emptied Himself on Calvary. Our Lord said that our cross must be borne if we are going to be His disciples. If we are not willing to bear our cross, we cannot be His disciple. This means emptying ourselves, pouring ourselves out for our dear Savior. The battle we fight is against ourselves. We think that the world revolves around us. We judge things by how they affect us. That attitude is not the attitude of a disciple. The attitude of a disciple involves cross-bearing, dying to self and following the Savior.

Discipleship

THE MISSION OF THE LORD

Very few passages of Scripture in the Bible are misinterpreted more often than this passage in Luke 14:28-30. Christ says,

> *For which of you, intending to build a tower, sitteth not down first, and counteth the cost, whether he have sufficient to finish it? Lest haply, after he hath laid the foundation, and is not able to finish it, all that behold it begin to mock him, saying, This man began to build, and was not able to finish.*

One hears many ideas about interpreting this passage and this parable. It is about a foolish person that did not take into account all that is involved in building. This foolish person started building and did not finish. That is not the point here. That is the farthest thing from the point.

The Bible says in Luke 14:31-33,

> *Or what king, going to make war against another king, sitteth not down first, and consulteth whether he be able with ten thousand to meet him that cometh against him with twenty thousand? Or else, while the other is yet a great way off, he sendeth an ambassage, and desireth conditions of peace. So likewise, whosoever he be of you that forsaketh not all that he hath, he cannot be my disciple.*

What is Christ talking about? He is speaking of His mission. If you are a builder, you do not want a crew of lazy men working for you. If you are a warrior and a captain in an army, and you are leading an army against the enemy, you do not want soldiers who will whine and cry and will not go to battle, or quit in the middle of the fight. The Lord Jesus turned and told the multitude that was walking after Him that unless they chose Him in the hour of great conflict and great testing, they could not be His disciples. Unless they chose Him over wife, father, mother, son, and daughter, they could not be His disciples. Unless they were willing to empty themselves, bearing their cross, they could not be His disciples.

> We should be with Him, building until it is done and battling until it is won.

The Lord Jesus said, "I am a builder. I am a warrior. If I am going to build what I must build, I must have people who will pay the price to build it. If I am going to wage war against the Devil, I must have warriors who will work with Me and stand with Me."

Do not complain about the cost of discipleship when you think about the mission of Christ. We should be with Him, building until it is done and battling until it is won. God's work is not something for cowards. It is not something for someone who wants to start and stop. It is not for someone who wants to watch like a spectator at a parade.

The Lord is the builder in this parable. The Lord is the captain in this parable. The Lord is saying, "I am going to build and I am going to wage war." The reason that this building has so little progress, and this war so little victory at times, is that we have not made as much of discipleship as we should have. Most churches are not challenged and stirred. The Lord saw this great multitude following Him and He said, "If you are going to be My disciple, you must choose Me over wife, mother, father, son, daughter, sister and brother. You must bear your cross. You must forsake all. There cannot be anything that you regard higher than you regard God. I have a building to build and a war to wage and I need this kind of person." This is the kind of church we must have. The strength of a church is not its size; the strength of a church is its likeness to Christ.

One of Charles Spurgeon's biographers tells the story of the first time Spurgeon and his future wife Susannah were together. It was at a preaching engagement. When the meeting had concluded, Spurgeon left without realizing that he had forgotten to take his guest with him when he exited the meeting. Later, Susannah said that she realized at that first meeting with her husband-to-be that she would always take second place in his life. The Lord Jesus would always be first.

The strength of a church is not its size; the strength of a church is its likeness to Christ.

Luke 14:26-27 says, *"If any man come to me, and hate not his father, and mother, and wife, and children, and brethren, and sisters, yea, and his own life also, he cannot be my disciple. And whosoever doth not bear his cross, and come after me, cannot be my disciple."*

Verse thirty-three says, *"So likewise, whosoever he be of you that forsaketh not all that he hath, he cannot be my disciple."* This causes us to wonder how few disciples the Lord has. It makes each of us think about whether we are disciples of Jesus Christ. He is building, He is battling. He must have this kind of person to build with Him and battle with Him.

THE MEN WHO HEAR HIM

The Bible says in Luke 14:34-35, *"Salt is good: but if the salt have lost his savour, wherewith shall it be seasoned? It is neither fit for the land, nor yet for the dunghill; but men cast it out. He that hath ears to hear, let him hear."*

Not everyone has ears to hear. *"He that hath ears to hear, let him hear."* Let us move to Luke 15:1-2, *"Then drew near unto him all the publicans and sinners for to hear him. And the Pharisees and scribes murmured, saying, This man receiveth sinners, and eateth with them."*

He put forth this kind of challenge, and the publicans and sinners said, "That's what we want. We know that we are nothing of ourselves. We know that we have nothing to offer except ourselves."

When this kind of challenge goes forth, we still have the same kind of response. There are people who say, "I want Him. I desire Him. I am nothing of myself; all I can give Him is me." There are others who say, "I'll find another way. I would rather have a weaker Christianity." They then begin to murmur and complain.

The reason that this building has so little progress, and this war so little victory at times, is that we have not made as much of discipleship as we should have.

We may read of the sacrifices of some people who changed the world; some of them were Communist leaders; some of them were godless people. What they were motivated by and what we are motivated by are two different things. Considering the sacrifices they made to change the world, it makes me wonder what Christians are willing to do. If He is who we say He is, if heaven and hell are real places, if Christ is the only way to heaven, then we should desire to do what He says in order to be His disciples.

The truth is, many of us are just kidding ourselves in thinking that we are serving Him. If we are going to build with Him and battle with Him, we must be willing to be His disciples.

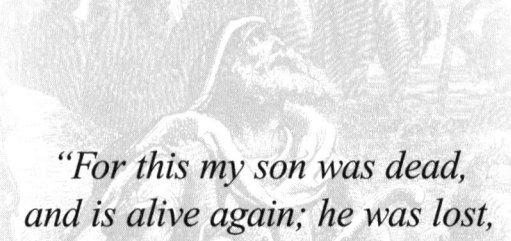

*"For this my son was dead,
and is alive again; he was lost,
and is found."*

Luke 15:24

Chapter Nine

THE LOST SHEEP, THE LOST COIN, AND THE LOST SON

On one occasion, when Christ was surrounded by publicans and sinners, He gave the amazing story recorded in Luke chapter fifteen. As Christ was seated with publicans and sinners, these outcasts looked down upon by society, the religious leaders accused Him of doing something wrong. They said, *"This man receiveth sinners, and eateth with them."* His accusers meant this to condemn Him, but it is one of the greatest compliments given to Christ. For had not Christ received sinners, no one could come to Him.

Leading up to this amazing story, we find that the Lord Jesus Christ said three times, *"He cannot be my disciple,"* in Luke chapter fourteen. What a stirring statement! In this passage we find a great multitude following Him. The Lord turned and faced the people and told them that unless they were willing to bear their cross, unless they were willing to hate father and mother (in other words, always choosing Christ even above family), unless they were willing to forsake all, they could not be His disciples. The building that must be done and the battle that must be won by the Lord required a certain type of person, and that person could not be His disciple without doing these things.

The Lord said, *"He that hath ears to hear, let him hear,"* and immediately we come to the fifteenth chapter of Luke. The Bible says in Luke 15:1-4,

> *Then drew near unto him all the publicans and sinners for to hear him. And the Pharisees and scribes murmured, saying, This man receiveth sinners, and eateth with them. And he spake this parable unto them, saying, What man of you, having an hundred sheep, if he lose one of them, doth not leave the ninety and nine in the wilderness, and go after that which is lost, until he find it?*

In verse nine the Bible says, *"And when she hath found it, she calleth her friends and her neighbours together, saying, Rejoice with me; for I have found the piece which I had lost."*

Again the Word of God says in verse twenty-four, *"For this my son was dead, and is alive again; he was lost, and is found. And they began to be merry."*

Note a word in verse four of Luke chapter fifteen. The word is *"lost."* The same word is in verse nine, *"lost."* This word is also in verse twenty-four, *"lost."* We normally look at this passage of Scripture in Luke chapter fifteen as containing three parables; but if you notice the language of the Scripture in verse three, the Bible says, *"And he spake this parable unto them, saying."* It would be correct to say that this is one parable unfolding three stories. It is a parable that teaches us the great love of God for the lost.

The Lost Sheep, the Lost Coin, and the Lost Son

Do you see yourself as a sinner? I want you to know that there is a Savior; His name is Jesus Christ. In spite of everything you have ever done or ever will do, God loves you. There is nothing you have done that has canceled His love. He longs for you to know Him and to know His great love for you.

It is a horrible thing to be lost. Some people are lost physically. For a while, they are separated from family or friends. Later, they are found, and everyone rejoices. Some people suffer financial loss. When individuals are going through financial troubles, they feel that it is one of the worst things that could possibly happen to them. Some people lose their minds. They can no longer think rationally. This is a great sorrow. But there is no loss that compares to the loss of the eternal soul.

The Lord Jesus came because people are lost. In Luke 19:10 the Bible says, *"For the Son of man is come to seek and to save that which was lost."* All of us that are saved were once lost. However, I think most of us have forgotten what it means to be lost. We have forgotten what it was like when we were convicted of our sin and knew that if we died we were going to go to a Devil's hell forever. In the blackness of darkness without God and without hope, we were lost.

In spite of everything you have ever done or ever will do, God loves you.

We see publicans, sinners, people in need, and the lost. There are two kinds of lost people here. There are those that know they are lost, and there are those who do not know. The latter group refuses to see themselves as lost, hell-bound, condemned sinners.

If someone listened to most of us talk, he would find that we talk more like the Pharisees than the publicans and sinners. We talk more like a crowd that does not understand what it means to be a sinner than we do like the crowd that does understand. Perhaps our problem is that we have drifted too far from the cross. We have forgotten what we were when the Lord found us. We have forgotten what He was willing to do to save us.

The Lord Jesus, seated with the publicans and sinners, condemned by the Pharisees, unfolds this parable containing three stories. In these stories we see God the Father, God the Son, and God the Holy Spirit.

THE LORD SEES US

Beginning in the first story, we discover that the Lord sees us. The Word of God says in Luke 15:1-7,

> *And he spake this parable unto them, saying, What man of you, having an hundred sheep, if he lose one of them, doth not leave the ninety and nine in the wilderness, and go after that which is lost, until he find it? And when he hath found it, he layeth it on his shoulders, rejoicing. And when he cometh home, he calleth together his friends and neighbours, saying unto them, Rejoice with me; for I have found my sheep which was lost. I say unto you, that likewise joy shall be in heaven over one sinner that repenteth, more than over ninety and nine just persons, which need no repentance.*

In this particular story, the Son of God, the Lord Jesus Christ, sees that there is one lost sheep. When the count is taken, there are only ninety-nine sheep. What is one? How could one mean so much? We must realize what one means to Christ. That one means so much that Jesus Christ did what He did for that one. Our Great Shepherd saw one lost sheep, where that lost sheep was, and what that lost sheep needed.

The Lost Sheep, the Lost Coin, and the Lost Son

In the second story, the Bible says in Luke 15:8-10,

> *Either what woman having ten pieces of silver, if she lose one piece, doth not light a candle, and sweep the house, and seek diligently till she find it? And when she hath found it, she calleth her friends and her neighbours together, saying, Rejoice with me; for I have found the piece which I had lost. Likewise, I say unto you, there is joy in the presence of the angels of God over one sinner that repenteth.*

The woman had ten coins. She saw that one of them was lost. She went after that one that was lost.

The Bible says in Luke 15:11-16,

> *And he said, A certain man had two sons: and the younger of them said to his father, Father, give me the portion of goods that falleth to me. And he divided unto them his living. And not many days after the younger son gathered all together, and took his journey into a far country, and there wasted his substance with riotous living. And when he had spent all, there arose a mighty famine in that land; and he began to be in want. And he went and joined himself to a citizen of that country; and he sent him into his fields to feed swine. And he would fain have filled his belly with the husks that the swine did eat: and no man gave unto him.*

There was a lost son and the Lord saw him lost. The Lord sees us. One of a hundred He sees. One of ten He sees. One of two He sees. One sheep He sees. One coin He sees. One son He sees.

Perhaps we need to hear again the words of Proverbs 15:3: *"The eyes of the Lord are in every place, beholding the evil and the good."*

The Parables of Jesus

There is nothing that we have ever done or ever shall do that God does not see. There are some things I am glad I do not see. There are things I am happy I do not know about others, and there are things that I am happy others do not know about me. However, there is nothing about anyone that God does not know and see.

There is nothing that God has not already seen, yet He loves us so. This thought overwhelms me. How ashamed I am at times in my life and how ashamed you must be. In the secret, private places where no one sees, in the thought life, in the corners of our mind where no one has walked, where we think no one sees–God sees. Yet He loves us with an everlasting love. How grateful we should be that our God sees and loves us.

THE LORD SEEKS US

Second, the Lord seeks us. The Bible says in Luke 15:4-6,

> *What man of you, having an hundred sheep, if he lose one of them, doth not leave the ninety and nine in the wilderness, and go after that which is lost, until he find it? And when he hath found it, he layeth it on his shoulders, rejoicing. And when he cometh home, he calleth together his friends and neighbours, saying unto them, Rejoice with me; for I have found my sheep which was lost. I say unto you, that likewise joy shall be in heaven over one sinner that repenteth, more than over ninety and nine just persons, which need no repentance.*

The first story is the story of the Son of God. This story is of the Great Shepherd of our souls and how He came to earth to find us. He sought us. His seeking took Him to Calvary. There was no way to find us apart from the cross. Jesus Christ was willing to come to earth, to be born of a virgin, to live a sinless life, and to suffer the humiliation of incarnation.

We speak often of the humiliation of the cross. Beyond what we can imagine, there was the humiliation as Christ hung on the cross before a jeering world while innocent of any crime, any sin of His own. The Sinless One hung there in the humiliation of Calvary. However, the humiliation of Calvary was preceded by the humiliation of His incarnation, as God was willing to become man. He was all God and all man, yet without sin. God became man without ceasing to be God. He was the sinless Son of God.

As I read God's Word more and more, I come to understand and know more of what it cost God to seek me. He gave His only begotten Son. The Lord Jesus went to Calvary and suffered our death, our payment, our penalty, our hell, and our separation from God. He was willing to do all that He did to seek us. Our loving Shepherd, who loved His sheep, was willing to face whatever foe He had to face, to go wherever He must go to find one that was lost. God seeks us.

Notice in the second story, *"Either what woman having ten pieces of silver, if she lose one piece, doth not light a candle, and sweep the house, and seek diligently till she find it?"* In this second story we see God the Holy Spirit. In the first story, the sheep is lost in the wilderness. In the second story, the coin is lost inside the house. The woman lights a candle. She penctrates the darkness. She sweeps and seeks diligently with a lighted candle until she finds it. She is seeking. This is the way the Holy Spirit works. He seeks us. He stays after us. There is no place we can hide from God. Many people have thought they could find somewhere in the world where they would not have to hear about God any longer, or where they would not have to hear people talk to them about God. It does not work this way. No matter where you are or where you go, God can find you. He seeks after us.

The Parables of Jesus

Many of us have had people we know and love disappear from our presence, and we wondered where they were and what they were doing. We suffered great anguish as we thought about them. Our hearts hurt as we thought about where they were and what they were doing and what they needed. We found relief, peace, and rest only as we came to the Lord and said, "Lord, I know You know where they are, and You are seeking them."

The third story we call the story of the prodigal son. It is more appropriately the story of the loving father.

There are some people suffering now, wondering about loved ones and where they may be or what they may be doing. We never find any peace, any relief, or any rest until we realize God is seeking after them. We must leave them in God's hands. The blessed Holy Spirit is trailing them. He is seeking them out just as surely as the woman sought the coin.

The Lord Jesus is giving all of this in a message not just to the Pharisees who have rebuked Him and ridiculed Him, but in tender love and compassion, He is assuring these publicans and sinners of how He cares for them.

The third story we call the story of the prodigal son. It is more appropriately the story of the loving father. When we say the parables of Jesus are the greatest stories ever told, this particular story of the son and the loving father is the greatest of the greatest stories ever told. It is the pearl, or crown, of all the parables.

The Bible says in Luke 15:11-19,

> *And he said, A certain man had two sons. And the younger of them said to his father, Father, give me the portion of goods that falleth to me. And he divided unto them his living. And not many days after the younger*

The Lost Sheep, the Lost Coin, and the Lost Son

son gathered all together and took his journey into a far country, and there wasted his substance with riotous living. And when he had spent all, there arose a mighty famine in that land; and he began to be in want. And he went and joined himself to a citizen of that country; and he sent him into his fields to feed swine. And he would fain have filled his belly with the husks that the swine did eat: and no man gave unto him. And when he came to himself, he said, How many hired servants of my father's have bread enough and to spare, and I perish with hunger! I will arise and go to my father, and I will say unto him, Father, I have sinned against heaven, and before thee, And am no more worthy to be called thy son: make me as one of thy hired servants.

What is occurring here? In the first story, we see a picture of God the Son; in the second, God the Holy Spirit. In this third story, we find God the Father. In this story, the son comes to the father and says, "I want what is coming to me." Because he was the younger of the sons, he received half of what the elder brother would have received. He then took his journey into a far country. A far country is any place where someone tries to escape God.

Happiness is not something we can find by seeking it. It is a by-product of following after the Lord and obeying Him. He gives us joy.

We must decide whether we are going to live under God's authority or whether we are going to serve the Devil. Everyone on the face of the earth has submitted to the authority of God or to the authority of the Devil. Some may have the idea they are serving themselves and doing as they please. However, there is no such thing. That is simply a convenient way for the Devil to let you get by with living for him by thinking that you are serving yourself.

The son in our story said, "No more rules for me. No more authority for me. I want what is coming to me. I am going to spend it as I please, live as I please, do as I please." That, my friend, is the *"far country."*

The Bible says, *"He wasted his substance."* How much of your life has been wasted? All of life away from God is wasted. But God seeks us. *"And he began to be in want."* Wasting life and wanting go hand in hand. It is interesting that the son left home with money in his pockets; he had everything that he needed. The son had his inheritance, but it was not long until he was in want.

Remember that long before you thought of seeking God, He was seeking you.

What this son needed was not an inheritance. What he needed was not material things. The son had a greater need, and no amount of material possessions could meet that need. Some people think that if they could have a new this or new that, it would make them happy. No, we are not going to be happy until we have a new heart. Happiness is not something we can find by seeking it. It is a by-product of following after the Lord and obeying Him. He gives us joy. The Lord uses these terms very carefully.

Luke 15:14 says, *"And when he had spent all, there arose a mighty famine in that land; and he began to be in want."* The *"mighty famine"* is God at work. *"And he went and joined himself to a citizen of that country; and he sent him into the fields to feed swine."* What a job for a Jew. Jews had nothing to do with that type of animal. The son had gone so far down that he was feeding swine. Not only was he feeding swine, he was ready to eat what the swine ate. *"And he would fain have filled his belly with the husks that the swine did eat:*

The Lost Sheep, the Lost Coin, and the Lost Son

and no man gave unto him." One has to wonder, "Where were his friends then?" When his money ran out, his friends ran out. Young people are not the only age group that needs to learn this lesson; there are many older people who need to learn this lesson also.

"And when he came to himself, he said, How many hired servants of my father's have bread enough and to spare, and I perish with hunger! I will arise and go to my father." Notice the intellect, *"He came to himself."* The son came to his right mind. Sin brings an insanity. There are people in sin who do things no one can explain. A man runs off with someone, leaving a beautiful wife and beautiful children. He leaves his home and everything he ever had. What happened to him? The Devil got him. He acts like an insane man. Like a fool, he is gone after strange flesh. That is what happened. He is out of his mind. One cannot explain it.

A woman leaves her children, her home, her husband, and walks out. When I was growing up, for every one woman who left her family, six hundred men were leaving. Just to understand what kind of world we are living in, the sides are now even. As many women leave their families and run away as do men. Our world has changed. We live in a world of unnatural affection.

The son came to himself and said, *"How many hired servants of my father's have bread enough and to spare, and I perish with hunger!"* He faced the facts, then he felt something. His emotions became involved. His will then became involved and he said, *"I will arise and go to my father."* The son rehearsed a speech. He said that when he got there he would tell his father that he did not deserve to be a son any longer. He was just going to be a servant. Why did all that happen? God was seeking him, and He seeks after us. Remember that long before you thought of seeking God, He was seeking you.

The Parables of Jesus

THE LORD SAVES US

The shepherd went after the one sheep until he found it. The woman sought for the coin until she found it.

The Bible says in Luke 15:20, *"And he arose, and came to his father. But when he was yet a great way off, his father saw him and had compassion, and ran and fell on his neck and kissed him."* The son did not have to run to his father. The father ran to the son. When the boy was a great way off, the father ran to the son. This is our heavenly Father.

> *A far country is any place where someone tries to escape God.*

When we say, "I will arise and go to Jesus," the Lord Jesus is there. At that moment, He is standing right there. Years ago, when I was a young preacher, I would talk about all the wicked things the boy in this story had to go back through, and what he had to do on his way back to his father. I made it a terrible trip back home, but I was wrong. It is not a terrible trip back home; it is a terrible trip to the far country. It is a wonderful, glorious trip back home to God. Our holy God makes us fully aware of the awfulness of our sin. When we see ourselves as God sees us and arise to go to the Father, we find Him with open arms to receive us.

When you say, "I'm coming to Jesus," the Lord Jesus is running to meet you. Our Lord wanted these poor, downcast sinners to know that He came to earth, He came all the way from glory, and He would meet them where they were.

What does a man have to do to get saved? He must repent of his sin and put his faith in Christ. He will not respond to the "good news" until he is fully aware of the "bad news" about his sin. As a matter of fact, the "good news" is no news at all until we have heard the "bad news" about our sinful condition apart from God. The Bible

The Lost Sheep, the Lost Coin, and the Lost Son

says the father ran to him and smothered him with kisses. Think a moment about the hog trough. Think about where the boy had been. It was not only the dirt and the slime of the hog trough or pig pen. This boy had been involved with everything imaginable. You name it, and he had experienced it. God saw it all.

I am very grateful to God that most people in our churches have been protected from this kind of life, but it does not give us any excuse to look down on those that have not been protected. There are people who are staggering through life with the luggage of wounds, sorrow, heartache, and hurt that is beyond what we can imagine. When they started out as little girls and boys, they did not have the opportunity that some people had.

Here is a boy no one wanted, but his father still loved him. Here is a boy with the stench of the hogs and every social disgrace imaginable on him, but his father still loved him. You may want to think about what you have done, but I want you to know that nothing you have ever done has canceled God's love for you. He loves you with an everlasting love. He yearns for you to come to Him. When you say, "I'm coming," you will find Him running to meet you. The Word of God says,

> *And he arose, and came to his father. But when he was yet a great way off, his father saw him, and had compassion, and ran, and fell on his neck and kissed him. And the son said unto him, Father, I have sinned against heaven, and in thy sight, and am no more worthy to be called thy son.*

The father stopped the son in the middle of his speech. He would not let him finish. He would not let the son say, *"Make me as one of thy hired servants."* God has not made us servants. We serve Him because we love Him. He has made us His own dear sons. He brought us into His own family. He made us heirs with God and joint

The Parables of Jesus

heirs with Jesus Christ. Heaven is my home. God is my Father. I serve Him because I love Him, but He has made me one of His sons. I have been born into His family.

The Bible says,

> But the father said to his servants, Bring forth the best robe, and put it on him; and put a ring on his hand, and shoes on his feet: and bring hither the fatted calf, and kill it; and let us eat, and be merry: for this my son was dead, and is alive again; he was lost, and is found. And they began to be merry.

What a day it was when that boy came home! Have you ever experienced anything like that? My mind goes back to the Lord Jesus and the publicans and sinners and the Pharisees talking about it. The Lord Jesus told them these stories. It is as though He whispered in tender compassion to those publicans and sinners and to the Pharisees, "God sees you. God seeks after you. God can save you."

"It was meet that we should make merry, and be glad: for this thy brother was dead, and is alive again; and was lost, and is found."

Luke 15:32

THE LOST SON WHO NEVER LEFT HOME

ou can travel into the "far country" and waste your life without ever leaving home. As our Lord sat with the publicans and sinners, the scribes and Pharisees criticized Him for receiving sinners and publicans. He gave them a parable that unfolded in three great stories, the last of which could be called the "crown of all the parables." It is commonly referred to as the parable of the prodigal son, but it would be more accurately called the story of the loving father. The Bible says in Luke 15:25-32,

> *Now his elder son was in the field: and as he came and drew nigh to the house, he heard musick and dancing. And he called one of the servants, and asked what these things meant. And he said unto him, Thy brother is come; and thy father hath killed the fatted calf, because he hath received him*

safe and sound. And he was angry, and would not go in: therefore came his father out, and intreated him. And he answering said to his father, Lo, these many years do I serve thee, neither transgressed I at any time thy commandment: and yet thou never gavest me a kid, that I might make merry with my friends: but as soon as this thy son was come, which hath devoured thy living with harlots, thou hast killed for him the fatted calf. And he said unto him, Son, thou art ever with me, and all that I have is thine. It was meet that we should make merry, and be glad: for this thy brother was dead, and is alive again; and was lost, and is found.

Remember in verse eleven the Bible says, *"And he said, A certain man had two sons."* Thinking of the elder brother, note the expression in the twenty-fifth verse, *"Now his elder son."* This parable could have concluded, very easily, with the story of the prodigal's return home, but we would always wonder about the other boy. So the Lord leaves us no room for doubt about the second son.

You can travel into the "far country" and waste your life without ever leaving home.

The Word of God says in Luke 15:1-3, *"Then drew near unto him all the publicans and sinners for to hear him. And the Pharisees and scribes murmured, saying, This man receiveth sinners, and eateth with them. And he spake this parable unto them, saying."*

Christ goes on with the story about a man with a hundred sheep who lost one. He sought that lost sheep until he found it. Then He tells the story of a woman with ten coins. She lost one of the coins, and she sought diligently until she found it. Then the Lord tells us

The Lost Son Who Never Left Home

about a father with two sons. One of the boys came to him and said, "I want what belongs to me, what is coming to me. My inheritance, that is what I want."

The father divided unto him his inheritance, which was half what the elder brother would have received. The Bible says that the younger left and went to the far country. He *"wasted his substance with riotous living."* The younger son came to a hog feeding place. Luke 15:17-19 says,

> *And when he came to himself, he said, How many hired servants of my father's have bread enough and to spare, and I perish with hunger! I will arise and go to my father, and will say unto him, Father, I have sinned against heaven and before thee, and am no more worthy to be called thy son: make me as one of thy hired servants.*

The son had a speech prepared, and he started home. The very next verse in the Bible says he came, and *"his father saw him, and had compassion, and ran, and fell on his neck, and kissed him."* His father called for a robe to be put upon him, a ring to be placed on his finger, and shoes to be placed on his feet. He ordered that the fatted calf be killed. I have an idea, just my idea, that the father was having that calf fattened for this occasion. He lived in expectation that his son was going to come home. This is what he wanted to do. Now it was time to kill the fatted calf and rejoice.

THE CONDITION OF THE ELDER BROTHER

As everyone was rejoicing in the house, coming in from the fields, the elder brother heard the sound of music. He would not go into the house, but rather called a servant and asked him why there was music. The servant, thinking that the brother would love to hear

The Parables of Jesus

the news said, *"Thy brother is come; and thy father hath killed the fatted calf, because he hath received him safe and sound."*

The Bible says the elder son became angry. He was so angry that he would not go inside to see his own father or embrace his brother. So they carried the news to the father that his other son was standing outside full of anger and would not come inside. He was angry about what had happened. So the father had to leave the celebration to come outside and deal with his other lost son. The younger son was lost in riotous living. His sin was expressed in that manner. The other was lost in self-righteousness. When the father came, he had a conversation with his son. Luke 15:28-32 says,

> *And he was angry, and would not go in: therefore came his father out, and intreated him. And he answering said to his father, Lo, these many years do I serve thee, neither transgressed I at any time thy commandment: and yet thou never gavest me a kid, that I might make merry with my friends: but as soon as this thy son was come, which hath devoured thy living with harlots, thou hast killed for him the fatted calf. And he said unto him, Son, thou art ever with me, and all that I have is thine. It was meet that we should make merry, and be glad: for this thy brother was dead, and is alive again; and was lost, and is found.*

Take note of some things here. He said, *"Thou never gavest me a kid."* In other words he said, "You never even killed a goat for me. You never had a celebration for me, not even so much as killing a goat for me. But he comes home, after he has wasted all his money and lived with harlots, and you killed the fatted calf for him."

Then the elder brother says, *"thy son."* He will not even claim him as his own brother. Notice the language here very specifically given in verse thirty. He says to his father,

The Lost Son Who Never Left Home

> *But as soon as this thy son was come, which hath devoured thy living with harlots, thou hast killed for him the fatted calf. And the father said unto him, Son, thou art ever with me, and all that I have is thine. It was meet that we should make merry, and be glad: for this thy brother was dead, and is alive again; and was lost, and is found.*

The boy said, *"thy son."* The father said, "Remember, he is not just my son, he is your brother."

This parable was to speak to the hearts of the scribes and Pharisees. There is no problem understanding that the shepherd in the first story is the Lord Jesus Christ, God's Son. The woman searching in the second story is a picture of the Holy Spirit of God seeking for our souls. There are other places in Scripture where the Spirit of God is referred to as feminine; not in gender, but in behavior. The Spirit of God is seen as brooding, caring. Even our Lord said, *"As a hen doth gather her brood under her wings."* There is a compassion that is tender. It is portrayed as the tender loving care of the Holy Spirit of God.

The younger son was lost in riotous living. His sin was expressed in that manner. The other was lost in self-righteousness.

In this story of the two boys, we have a picture of our heavenly Father that *"so loved the world, that he gave his only begotten Son, that whosoever believeth in him should not perish, but have everlasting life"* (John 3:16). The father races to his son and embraces him and cares for him. We have no problem understanding the love of God when we see Christ seated with the publicans and sinners, the outcasts, the rejected of society. We have no problem understanding which person in these three stories represents the Lord. We have no problem understanding from these stories how these publicans and sinners, these outcasts, are represented in the sheep that was lost, and the prodigal that was gone from home. But we understand that Christ was talking about these scribes and Pharisees when He deals with this elder brother. It is my opinion that Christ looked them right in the eye when He started this part of the story and told them this story of the elder brother.

When I read and study this portion of Scripture, my heart hurts as I think of my own sin, my self-righteousness, my pharisaical attitude, my holier-than-thou attitude. And my heart also hurts for you because there are many of you who have this pharisaical attitude. It is demonstrated in the way we live and in the attitude we have toward people. May God help us to come clean with the Lord on this matter.

We see this life, this pharisaical attitude, expressed when this son, this brother, could not rejoice in the salvation of a lost soul. Everyone else was thrilled because the boy had come home. They were making merry. There was music being played. They had killed the fatted calf. There was such a festive spirit. They had every reason in the world to be excited. They had prayed, and God had answered their prayers; something wonderful had taken place, not only on earth, but *"there is joy in the presence of the angels of God over one sinner that repenteth."*

However, there was someone who could not rejoice. He did not get excited about it. Other things excited him, but not the sight of seeing someone saved. We get concerned about so many things other than the salvation of souls.

Some people attend church regularly, go through all the motions, do everything like the elder brother said he did, but do not get excited at all about people coming to Christ. They have the same attitude that the elder brother had. He wanted a fatted calf for himself; he wanted a kid for himself.

The Lost Son Who Never Left Home

The kind of church we want is one that is excited about people getting saved. It is the kind of church where people rejoice and praise God that others are coming to Christ. God is not pleased when we are not excited about people coming to Christ. There is nothing so close to the heart of God as rejoicing over the salvation of sinners. There is nothing so far removed from the heart of God, and so much like Satan, as the lack of rejoicing over the salvation of souls.

This boy said, "I have been out in the field. I have been here all of my life. I have never done anything wrong. I have done exactly what I am supposed to do. I have been here working hard." That is commendable. "I have been right in my place. You cannot find fault with me." One could not find fault in those things, but this son could not rejoice over his own brother coming to the Lord. That is the attitude of these Pharisees and scribes.

The second thing I see about this elder brother is that he cared more for things than he did for people. He was very upset that this younger brother had wasted all of his money. In a way, He was saying, "Pretty expensive lesson to learn." Luke 15:28-30 says,

> *And he was angry, and would not go in: therefore came his father out, and entreated him. And he answering said to his father, Lo, these many years do I serve thee, neither transgressed I at any time thy commandment: and yet thou never gavest me a kid, that I might make merry with my friends. But as soon as this thy son was come, which hath devoured thy living with harlots, thou hast killed for him the fatted calf.*

The greatest concern of this elder brother was that the younger brother threw all their father's money away. There comes a time when we should say, "Be thrifty. Do not waste your money. Take care of things. Have a certain kind of pride about the way things are done; make it look right." But if we ever get so in love with buildings and property that we forget about people, we are far removed from the Lord Jesus.

You may have a child, and you may say of that child, "He has wasted or she has wasted thousands." I am sorry. I truly am. I wish it could have been some other way. But if he has come to God, thank the Lord for this victory. You have gained a son, gained a daughter, gained someone you love. God brought this person home. Start celebrating and rejoicing over what God has done.

There is nothing so close to the heart of God as rejoicing over the salvation of sinners. There is nothing so far removed from the heart of God, and so much like Satan, as the lack of rejoicing over the salvation of souls.

Some folks have lost their ability to rejoice over anything. This older brother equated behavior with worth. We are all guilty of this. I am glad God does not think this way. The elder son said, "I have been a good boy. I have been doing everything I am supposed to do. I have kept all of your commandments. I have worked every day. I am actually out in the field working while they are having a party. I am out here slaving. I am a son, but I live like a servant. I am the good person, and your younger son is the bad person. I have done good, so I am good."

We make a mistake when we equate what people are worth with how they behave. In the eyes of God, they are all precious. Of course, this story brings to mind the grief we feel because of sin and the heart we should have for those that are sinners.

The Lost Son Who Never Left Home

THE COMPASSION OF THE FATHER

The elder son made another mistake. He kept the father's law, but he did not have the father's heart. Now we are talking about the Lord and what pleases Him. I spend a good deal of time preaching to myself. I want the property to look right and the buildings to look right; I want people to do right and be right. And by the way, there is nothing wrong with that, but that is not the goal. It is possible to live by the Law, do everything by the letter, and still not have the heart of the Lord.

The Bible says in Romans 7:6, *"But now we are delivered from the law, that being dead wherein we are held; that we should serve in newness of spirit, and not in the oldness of the letter."* God uses the Law to show us we need Him. But the Christian life is more than dos and don'ts. If you fuss all the time about the dos and don'ts, you have a bigger problem. The Christian life is a holy life. We are to be holy people, but holy people have a heart for God. Because of this, they have a passion for the souls of men.

In II Corinthians 3:6 the Bible says, *"Who also hath made us able ministers of the new testament; not of the letter, but of the spirit: for the letter killeth, but the spirit giveth life."* Was there anything wrong with that older boy going to work every day? No! Let us applaud him. That is great. Well, is there anything wrong with his staying around the house? No! That is commendable. There was nothing wrong with his order, his routine, his service; but he lived in the far country while he was at home. His "far country" was his self-righteousness.

> *We make a mistake when we equate what people are worth with how they behave. In the eyes of God, they are all precious.*

Some of us have tried to be good people, have tried to live the right kind of life, but we have developed an attitude that we are better than others who have not. As a matter of fact, we are a cut above them. To think that way is sin. There is nothing else you can call it.

I do not want anyone going out to do wrong, but it is possible to have the Law of the Father, to live by the letter of the Father, and not have the Father's heart. This is a matter where the Lord deals with me. To love the unlovely takes the grace of God. This is not routine; it is going beyond our normal duty.

What would you have said if you came out and talked with this boy? I know that I would have said, "Look! Can't you rejoice that your brother has come home? You are nothing but a hypocrite yourself. Look at you. You are filled with anger. You are so mad you won't even come in. Here we are inside having a grand time. Everybody should be in there rejoicing. Here you are acting as if you are not part of the family." This is the thing that proves we have the pharisaical attitude. The Lord Jesus Christ was just as tender with the elder son as He was with the prodigal son. The father spoke kindly to him. Let us read the conversation again. He is warning him. The Bible says in Luke 15:31-32,

> *And he said unto him, Son, thou art ever with me, and all that I have is thine. It was meet that we should make merry, and be glad: for this thy brother was dead, and is alive again; and was lost, and is found.*

THE CONCLUSION OF THE MATTER

Christ brings this entire chapter, this crowning story, this pearl of the parables, to this grand climactic statement in verse thirty-one.

The Lost Son Who Never Left Home

Do not miss it. Remember the scene. Christ is with sinners and publicans, and the scribes and Pharisees criticize Him. The beautiful story unfolds. A father had two sons. The love of the father is demonstrated as we see him rushing to his prodigal son. The father is warning the older son that he was falling into the same trap that his brother fell into. The younger son said, "I want what is mine. Give me what belongs to me."

The older brother had said, "You never gave me even a kid. You never gave me a fatted calf." Is that all he wants? Does he just want something from his father? Verse thirty-one says, *"And he said unto him, Son, thou art ever with me, and all that I have is thine."* Think of this, *"all that I have is thine."* We spend our lives thinking about what we can get from God, but God says, "Is it not enough that thou art ever with me?"

We argue and fuss about things. We allow things to upset us. We think of things we are being deprived of, something somebody gets that we do not get. We think our children are deprived of things that other children get. We murmur and complain, and we are all guilty. We gripe about what we do not have.

Do you realize that this would not even be a part of our thinking if we were satisfied with the Lord Jesus as we should be? *"Thou art ever with me."* The father is declaring, "I have more than fatted calves. I have more than kids. I have more than what I gave to your brother. I have more than some things. Everything I have is thine."

Can you imagine that we have a God in heaven who has made us heirs and joint heirs with Jesus Christ? He has brought us into His family and said, "It is all for you. All that I have is thine. Thou art ever with Me. All that I have is thine."

We may say that we are Christians, but do you know when we are the best Christians? We are the best Christians when we are walking so near the Lord that our happiness, our joy, our satisfaction are all found in Him. Let me illustrate this. I love my wife and love being with her. My wife does many things for me. As a matter of fact, she does every imaginable thing you can think a wife could do. But I would be foolish and you would know that I was foolish to say the reason I want her is so that she could prepare toast and eggs and oatmeal and iron my clothes. It is more than what we could get from one another or do for one another. It is loving her for who she is and caring for her because I love her.

We spend our lives thinking about what we can get from God, but God says, "Is it not enough that thou art ever with me?"

The Lord declares in this story that it is not trying to get a fatted calf or a party in your honor. Can you not see beyond that? *"Thou art ever with me..."* Is that not enough? *"...and all that I have is thine."* Is that not enough? If we really got hold of what we have in Christ and walked with God as we should walk with God, we would never murmur about things because we would be content with the Lord Jesus. We are saved sinners and heaven is our home. We are going to escape hell, and we have God's mercy and grace. I love this story because it tells of the love of God, and I love this story because it points out my sinfulness and my wrong attitude. I want God to help me find my complete joy and satisfaction in the Person of Jesus Christ.

"He that is faithful in that which is least is faithful also in much: and he that is unjust in the least is unjust also in much."

Luke 16:10

The Faithful

s it possible that God could give a test with only one question, and the answer to that one question would reveal everything about your life? Yes. The one question on the test would be, "Are you faithful in that which is least?" What we do with what we consider least reveals what we are doing with what God considers most.

It takes some thought to understand this parable. Once understood, a great lesson is learned. The purpose of a parable is not to teach many things, but to give one great truth God has for us in that parable.

The one great truth of this parable is found when we deal with the one great question concerning what we do with that which is least. What we do with that which is least reveals everything else about our lives. What do we do with that which is least?

The Parables of Jesus

Notice what the Word of God says in verse ten of Luke chapter sixteen, *"He that is faithful in that which is least is faithful also in much."*

The Bible says in Luke 16:1-13,

> *And he said also unto his disciples, There was a certain rich man, which had a steward; and the same was accused unto him that he had wasted his goods. And he called him, and said unto him, How is it that I hear this of thee? give an account of thy stewardship; for thou mayest be no longer steward. Then the steward said within himself, What shall I do? for my lord taketh away from me the stewardship: I cannot dig; to beg I am ashamed. I am resolved what to do, that, when I am put out of the stewardship, they may receive me into their houses. So he called every one of his lord's debtors unto him, and said unto the first, How much owest thou unto my lord? And he said, An hundred measures of oil. And he said unto him, Take thy bill, and sit down quickly, and write fifty. Then said he to another, And how much owest thou? And he said, An hundred measures of wheat. And he said unto him, Take thy bill, and write fourscore. And the lord commended the unjust steward, because he had done wisely: for the children of this world are in their generation wiser than the children of light. And I say unto you, Make to yourselves friends of the mammon of unrighteousness; that, when ye fail, they may receive you into everlasting habitations. He that is faithful in that which is least is faithful also in much: and he that is unjust in the least is unjust also in much. If therefore ye have not been faithful in the unrighteous mammon, who will commit to your trust the true*

> riches? And if ye have not been faithful in that which is another man's, who shall give you that which is your own? No servant can serve two masters: for either he will hate the one, and love the other; or else he will hold to the one, and despise the other. Ye cannot serve God and mammon.

The parable, as far as the story is concerned, seems quite easy to understand. Notice what the Bible says in Luke 16:1, *"And he said also unto his disciples, There was a certain rich man, which had a steward; and the same was accused unto him that he had wasted his goods."* This rich man had a steward. A steward is one who manages another's property, finances, or other affairs. It is similar to the office Joseph held in Egypt, except this particular steward did not have the character of Joseph. Everything about this man was dishonest. The only decent thing recorded of the steward is that he was willing to admit that he was too proud to beg. His master heard that he had wasted everything; he had sinned against his master. Most people are willing to do things with other people's money, goods, and time that they would not do with their own.

The master told the steward that he had been accused of wasting everything in his charge. The steward knew that he had been caught and would be relieved of his stewardship, so he devised a plan. He said, "I am going to find everyone who is indebted to my lord, and I am going to find out what they owe. When I find out what they owe, I am going to cut a deal with them."

So he asked one man, "How much do you owe?" The man told him, and the steward said, "All right, pay fifty percent of it." He said to another man, "How much do you owe?" The man told him, and he said, "Pay eighty percent of it."

The Parables of Jesus

The steward's lord commended the man for his quick response, but he still lost his job because he acted dishonestly. The steward was without employment because he did not do the right thing.

The word *parable* means "to place alongside." The Lord Jesus took this story and placed alongside it the great lesson we are to learn as His children.

Keep in mind that Christ was on His way to Calvary. His earthly ministry was drawing to a close. There is an intensity about this particular parable that we need to understand.

OUR FINANCES

The first thing we must consider is our finances, because that is the theme of the parable. Notice in verse one of Luke chapter sixteen, *"And he said also unto his disciples."* Christ was speaking to His disciples. There were others who heard Him, but this was meant for His disciples. He said, *"There was a certain rich man."* Note the expression *"rich man"* in verse one.

> *The attitude that God's children have toward finances should not be the same attitude the world has toward finances.*

At the end of verse fourteen of Luke chapter sixteen, the Bible says, *"And the Pharisees also, who were covetous, heard all these things: and they derided him."* In other words, the Pharisees were listening to the lesson the Lord gave to His disciples. The Bible said of the Pharisees who were listening to Christ that they craved money. They craved riches. They lived for finances. So Christ told about a certain rich man.

At the beginning of Luke chapter fifteen, the Lord Jesus was surrounded by publicans and sinners and the Pharisees came upon the scene and criticized Christ. He told one parable unfolding in three stories. He told the first story of a shepherd who had a hundred sheep, one of which was lost. The shepherd went and found the lost sheep. Christ then told about a woman who had ten coins, one of which was lost. She searched inside diligently until she found it. He told the third story about a father who had two sons. One son was lost out in the far country, and one was lost at home. We have no doubt about whom the Lord was talking when He told this parable.

In the first story of the lost sheep, the seeker is God the Son; the seeker in the second story is God the Holy Spirit; the seeker in the third story is God the Father. God the Son, God the Holy Spirit, and God the Father were seeking after sinners. There is no problem understanding who the lost were, because the lost were represented in the publicans and sinners who had gathered around the Lord Jesus.

In the story of the elder brother who would not rejoice over the salvation and the homecoming of his own brother, Christ was speaking of the hypocrites, the Pharisees, who did not rejoice over the prodigal coming home. They could not rejoice that the publicans and sinners were coming to Christ.

Notice the first word in the sixteenth chapter of Luke, *"And."* It is connected to the previous chapter. The Lord did not stop talking. He told the story about the lost sheep, the lost coin, the lost boy, and the elder brother. He then told the story of the rich man. It is all connected, and it continues in Luke 16:19-24,

> *There was a certain rich man, which was clothed in purple and fine linen, and fared sumptuously every day: and there was a certain beggar named Lazarus, which was laid at his gate, full of sores, and desiring to be fed with the crumbs which fell from the rich man's table: moreover the dogs came and licked his*

> *sores. And it came to pass, that the beggar died, and was carried by the angels into Abraham's bosom: the rich man also died, and was buried; and in hell he lift up his eyes, being in torments, and seeth Abraham afar off, and Lazarus in his bosom. And he cried and said, Father Abraham, have mercy on me, and send Lazarus, that he may dip the tip of his finger in water, and cool my tongue; for I am tormented in this flame.*

This is a continuation of this same lesson that Christ gave. He said, *"A certain rich man."* He talked of the Pharisees desiring riches and then in verse nineteen, He said there was another *"certain rich man."* Christ told His disciples of the difference between the way they lived and the way His followers should live. He told them about the attitude the Pharisees had toward finances and the attitude that His followers should have toward finances.

The attitude that God's children have toward finances should not be the same attitude the world has toward finances. What we do with the least of things in this world is the indicator of what we do with God. There is nothing immoral about the money; as a matter of fact, it is amoral. It is neither sinful nor good. What we do with it becomes the issue.

Consider I Timothy 6:6-7, *"But godliness with contentment is great gain. For we brought nothing into this world, and it is certain we can carry nothing out."* We know we came into this world with nothing but our naked souls, and we must realize that we are going out with nothing but our naked souls. We will meet God with absolutely nothing in our pockets. We are going to leave it all. The Bible says in I Timothy 6:8-10,

> *And having food and raiment let us be therewith content. But they that will be rich fall into temptation and a snare, and into many foolish and hurtful lusts,*

which drown men in destruction and perdition. For the love of money is the root of all evil: which while some coveted after, they have erred from the faith, and pierced themselves through with many sorrows.

The love of money, not money, is the root of all evil. People will sometimes misquote this verse by saying, "Money is the root of all evil." That is not what the Bible says. The Word of God says, *"The love of money is the root of all evil."*

There is some money we should not receive. For instance, a man came to me one day and said, "I want you to take a certain person into the Christian academy. If you will, I will build a building for you." The person he wanted to be admitted to our school had been in serious trouble with drugs and was not ready for such a school. You might be thinking, "Well, you are a man of principle. You are a man of integrity. You are a man of honesty. You are a man who cannot be bought." We need buildings, but I have to remind myself that God must give them. The man was asking, I believe, out of a heart of love. He had strong feelings toward someone he wanted me to help, but he wanted me to do something that was against everything we stand for. He was a very wealthy man. He let me know what he would do in return if I helped him. I felt that, though there is no evil in the money itself, it would have been evil for me to take that money. It was wrongly motivated. Once again, it is not the money, it is what we do with the money. What are we going to do with our finances?

What we do with the least of things in this world is the indicator of what we do with God.

The Parables of Jesus

OUR FRIENDSHIPS

The Bible says in verse eight of Luke chapter sixteen, *"And the lord commended the unjust steward, because he had done wisely: for the children of this world are wiser than the children of light."* Many times this verse of Scripture is taken out of context and people try to prove a little of everything with it. Note the two words in verse eight, *"their generation."* Understand what it really means. The children of this world are, in their generation, wiser in dealing with this world and their worldly or earthly things, than the children of light are, many times, in dealing with heavenly things.

The Word of God says in Luke 16:9, *"And I say unto you, Make to yourselves friends of the mammon of unrighteousness."* Does this sound like an evil thing? Remember, Jesus Christ is speaking here. Our Lord could not be instructing us to use evil means, evil motives, or evil methods.

The little word *"of"* means "by means of." The Word of God says, *"And I say unto you, Make to yourselves friends of..."* We use this word as meaning, "by means of" the mammon of unrighteousness. In other words, use money by means of the mammon of unrighteousness that when you fail, or die, *"they may receive you into everlasting habitations."*

Consider the connection between the expressions *"their houses"* in verse four to *"everlasting habitations"* in verse nine. There is a contrast. There is contrast between the way the Pharisees were living and what they were appearing to represent. The Pharisees claimed to be the spiritual leaders, the spiritual guides for all the people.

The story of the steward who used every means for his own advantage represents the Pharisees. The steward decided to steal from his lord. The lord rightly deserved one hundred percent, but the steward decided to steal fifty percent by telling the people who owed

that they only had to pay fifty percent. The steward stole twenty percent from the lord by telling others they only had to pay eighty percent of what they owed. The steward did not care about the lord. The only person he cared about was himself. He used any means to get ahead. The steward wanted people to receive him when he was dismissed from this job. He knew the people would receive him because he had let them off the hook and had not made them pay everything they owed the lord. He used the money to his own advantage so he could be welcomed into their homes.

We may want to stand in condemnation of this steward, but we must realize how often we do things the same way. We plan, scheme, and work to get things done our way and get things for ourselves and have people indebted to us. We do this with no thought of God, no thought of God's blessing, no thought of God's reward, no thought of the real Christian life, no thought of living for the Lord. We have taken the whole matter into our own hands. We are guilty.

Christ was teaching His disciples not to be tempted to use means to better themselves. He was teaching them that they must trust God to take care of them. Christ did not want the disciples to manipulate people like the Pharisees manipulated people. He did not want them to lie to people like the Pharisees lied to people. He did not want them to pretend to be something they were not like these Pharisees pretended to be something they were not. The Pharisees were interested only in their own gain. We do not have to be overcome by trying to get in this world. If we will faithfully serve Him, God will take care of us. If we have our faith right, our finances will be right. It makes no difference what may appear to people; if our faith is not right, our finances are not going to be right.

Christ was saying, "by means of the money." He was saying, "Use the money for the cause of Christ to win friends." This does not mean to win friends to yourselves, but to the Lord. When we die, they receive us, but the Bible says they receive us *"into everlasting habitations."* What does this mean? This means that while we are on earth, we are not to do what the self-righteous Pharisees did, living for self and giving to everything in order to get. This means that we do not try to make a name for ourselves or have people indebted to us. What we do with the money and the finances that God places in our hands is give it to the cause of Christ. By means of that mammon, you win people to the Lord Jesus. When we die, they will welcome us into heaven, and they will rejoice because we helped get them there by giving to the cause of Christ. This is what He was telling His disciples.

We spend so much of our time trying to get people to do the right things instead of spending time helping people be the right people.

Think how little we give. Of course, it is just money. It is not moral or immoral; it is amoral. What do you do with it? Do you give it to a missionary? Do you buy gospel tracts? Do you help spread the gospel with it? Money becomes a very sacred thing when it is given for these reasons because it is used to do a very sacred thing, winning people to Jesus Christ. When you die, and you have used your money for eternity, the people you won to Christ are going to welcome you into heaven and say, "Thank God you gave; I got saved because of it." This is what it is all about. It is not about living for this world so we can be entertained in their houses and get things while here on earth. That is not the way it is supposed to be.

The Lord Jesus told them they would be tempted to live just as the Pharisees lived, to do with their finances what the Pharisees did. The Pharisees were covetous. Christ told them of a certain rich man. He then told them about another rich man who went to hell. He wanted the people who craved money to get the message.

If you think being in the Lord's work delivers you from this temptation, you are wrong. With whom are you trying to make friends? There is someone on a mission field you have never seen. There is someone on an island of the sea you have never seen. He cannot do anything for you here on this earth. He cannot do you any favors down here. He cannot be indebted to you down here. He does not even know you. There are people we have never seen, never known, but we gave to get the gospel to them. We used the money God put in our hands to get the message of Christ to them. They are going to welcome us into glory and say, "I want you to know, I thank God that you gave and I got saved." They will welcome us into their *"eternal habitations."* This is a wonderful story!

OUR FAITH

The Bible says, *"He that is faithful in that which is least is faithful also in much: and he that is unjust in the least is unjust also in much."* Note the word, *"is."* One must discern what is least and what is much. There is a vital connection between what we do at this moment and what we do for eternity.

When our Lord talks about least and much, what do you imagine He is talking about? Can a Christian see what is least the same way a lost person sees what is least? Can a Christian judge what is most important the same way an unsaved person judges what is most important? Absolutely not. Through eyes of faith, one is to see the difference between the least and the much. We are talking about the least being the things of this earth, and the much being the things that are heavenly. The things that are least are the things of earth; the things that are most are things that are in heavenly view. If that be true, the verse may be interpreted like this: "He that is faithful in that which is of the earth is faithful also in the things of the heavenly view: and he that is unjust in the things that are put in our hands on this earth, things that are least, is unjust in that which is much."

Most of us, if not all of us, start out thinking, "I am going to be faithful in the least and then work my way up to the much." This is not what the Bible teaches. The Bible teaches just the opposite. The Bible teaches that as we do right with what is least, we are doing what is right with the much. If we take care of the heavenly view, we will automatically do what is right with the least.

Look at the little word *"is."* The Bible says, *"He that is faithful in that which is least is faithful also in much."* It does not say "will be" or "going to be" or "will surely be." He is already faithful in much. That is why he is faithful in the least. We spend so much of our time trying to get people to do the right things instead of spending time helping people be the right people. The right person is going to do the right thing. A person who is right with God and loves the Lord is going to do the right thing with what God places in his hand. We spend so much time talking to people about the result or the fruit, and so little time talking about the root. It should be just the opposite.

The Lord Jesus was saying, "You see these hypocrites gathered around Me. The publicans and sinners need to be saved. They are lost just like the sheep that was lost, like the coin that was lost, like the boy that was lost. These Pharisees care nothing for the lost. They are hypocrites. They care only about the things of this world and the riches of this world. They want to be seen of men like they are doing something special with this world, but they are not right with God. If they were right with God, they would automatically do what is right with the things of this earth." Christ instructed His disciples not to be like the Pharisees.

I once had a conversation with a young preacher who poured out his heart to me. As he talked to me, I discerned that he was a man who loved God. Like all of us, he had done some things, no doubt, that he should not have done, but he had a genuine heart for God. He asked me what he should do about some matters. I concluded from our conversation that he did not need to worry about whether he was

going to do the right thing or not, because he had a genuine heart for God. I am confident that, if he keeps that same heart, he is going to do the right thing.

Our Lord was saying, "Do not pretend. Do not play. Do not put on an act. Do not live for people who may be watching you. This is the way the Pharisees live; this is not the way to live. I want My followers to live as unto God."

Friends, what do we do with the least? Consider your wallet or checkbook. When you look at your checking account, what does it tell? Have you supported the Lord's work? When God puts something in your hand, what do you do with it? You see, by what we do with earthly things, "the least," we give evidence of whether or not we have faith toward God.

The Bible says in Luke 16:11-13,

> *If therefore ye have not been faithful in the unrighteous mammon, who will commit to your trust the true riches? And if ye have not been faithful in that which is another man's, who shall give you that which is your own? No servant can serve two masters: for either he will hate the one, and love the other; or else he will hold to the one, and despise the other. Ye cannot serve God and mammon.*

The Bible says, *"Ye cannot serve God and mammon."* The person who serves God will use the mammon, the things of this earth, for God's glory. The person who serves mammon will attempt to use God for his own gain, his own advantage.

The Lord told the disciples about a real hell. There are people who live and die and go to a real hell. They suffer conscious, unending torment in a real hell. We do not live here forever. When we die, the only way to miss hell and get to heaven is by repenting of our sin and trusting Jesus Christ for salvation.

The Lord was saying to His disciples, "If you really believe this, you will not live a pretentious life on earth; you will live a genuine Christian life, allowing God to be God of your life and using what God places in your hands for His glory. There will be proof of a genuine Christian life by what you do with the least, by what you do with the earthly."

Let us apply this to the church. Is your church a spiritual church? Is it a spiritual church because certain songs are sung or certain themes are sounded out? Does that give evidence that the people are spiritual people? No! The evidence of being a spiritual church is in what we do with what God puts in our hands. It is believing that there is a real heaven and a real hell and that Jesus Christ is the only way to heaven. By what we do with what God puts in our hands on this earth, we have proven whether or not we believe the Lord.

As God speaks to our hearts, all of us should come more in line with what the Lord desires for us to do and how He desires for us to live while we are on this earth. May God help us.

"And the publican, standing afar off, would not lift up so much as his eyes unto heaven, but smote upon his breast, saying, God be merciful to me a sinner."

Luke 18:13

Chapter Twelve

MERCY

o you recognize the need for mercy in your life? The testimony of John Newton, the former slave trader who became the famous hymn writer, is given in his hymn "Amazing Grace."

'Twas grace that taught my heart to fear,

And grace my fears relieved;

How precious did that grace appear,

The hour I first believed.

We witness God's amazing grace and mercy at work in the story of two very needy men who went to a place of prayer. Both went to pray, but only one of them left with his life changed. At first glance, if you had to choose one of the two men for a neighbor, it would not be a difficult choice to make. But let us examine the entire story more closely. The Lord Jesus said in Luke 18:9-14,

> *And he spake this parable unto certain which trusted in themselves that they were righteous, and despised others: two men went up into the temple to pray; the one a Pharisee, and the other a publican. The Pharisee stood and prayed thus with himself, God, I thank thee, that I am not as other men are, extortioners, unjust, adulterers, or even as this publican. I fast twice in the week, I give tithes of all that I possess. And the publican, standing afar off, would not lift up so much as his eyes unto heaven but smote upon his breast, saying, God be merciful to me a sinner. I tell you this man went down to his house justified rather than the other: for every one that exalteth himself shall be abased; and he that humbleth himself shall be exalted.*

The publican cried out, *"God be merciful to me a sinner."* Is that the way you feel about yourself? Can your name be put there? "God be merciful to Clarence Sexton, a sinner." Or in reality, do we find ourselves like the other man who said, *"I thank thee, that I am not as other men are"*? If we are honest, we most often talk and act like the Pharisee.

THE REASON

Notice the reason that the Lord gave this parable. The Bible says in Luke 18:9, *"And he spake this parable unto certain which trusted in themselves that they were righteous, and despised others."* These two things go hand in hand; when we believe that we are righteous,

we despise others. We have one standard we use for ourselves and another standard that we use for others.

The Lord Jesus gave this parable because of people who *"trusted in themselves."* Without exception, those of us who are Christians have trusted in the Lord Jesus Christ for our salvation. We have trusted Christ and Christ alone; we have asked Him to forgive our sin, and by faith we have received Him as our Savior.

It is wonderful to know that if you are a Christian you have eternal life. If you have confessed to God that you are a sinner, asked God to forgive your sin, and by faith received the Lord Jesus as your personal Savior, you are one of His children.

We say that we have trusted in Christ and Christ alone for salvation. Friends, we must trust in Christ and Christ alone to live the Christian life day by day also. Faith is not something we had and left. When we start to live the Christian life in our own energy, our own strength, our own deeds, then we start looking down at other people.

Jesus Christ said, *"Two men."* That is the way heaven viewed them both, just plainly, two men. *"Two men went up in to the temple to pray; the one a Pharisee, and the other a publican."* God said that they were both men, but what a contrast in their lives.

The Pharisee was a very religious man. One writer said that there were approximately three thousand Pharisees at that particular time. The Pharisees were very religious. They practiced the law; they lived a certain way, and they wanted everyone to know it. If one thinks that all of them were bad, think about Nicodemus. He came to the Lord Jesus under the cover of darkness. In John chapter three, the Bible tells of the conversation Christ had with Nicodemus. Think about Paul. The Bible calls him *"a Pharisee of the Pharisees."*

Remember that the Lord Jesus said this man trusted in himself. When we consider that, we realize that many of us have a pharisaical attitude.

The Parables of Jesus

The other man was a publican. In order to understand the parable, we should understand the background regarding the position the publican held in Jewish society. The Jews lived under the yoke of Roman bondage. Rome ruled the world. There were places in this world where Rome ruled that were more easily ruled than others. But there was one particular place that was very difficult to rule; it was in this Holy Land where the Jews lived and had their place of worship.

These two things go hand in hand; when we believe that we are righteous, we despise others.

The Jews felt they had their own ruler, and their ruler was God. They wanted to live in a type of theocracy and be ruled only by God; yet there was a civil government over them, the government of Rome. There was always conflict between the religious rule and the political rule of Rome.

There were many, many Jews who hated every notion that any people ruled them. Many despised the idea that the Roman eagle on the flag of Rome flew over their heads and that they were ruled and governed by Rome. The Jews wanted to do their own business, their own way, in their Jewish religion.

Can you imagine one of those Jews hiring himself out to the Roman government to work against his own people as a tax collector? And just so he would do a good job, the Roman government told him that he could keep a portion of what he collected. The more one collected, the more he could keep. So these publicans, or tax collectors, were Jews who worked for Rome; of course, they were despised and referred to as the most despicable people on the face of the earth. No respectable Jew wanted anything to do with a publican. The publicans were known for their criminal behavior and the awful things they did. When gathering taxes, they would go to any length to enrich their own coffers.

Here was a respectable Pharisee. Like a Nicodemus, like a Paul, he was a respectable Pharisee who walked into the temple to pray. Also coming to the temple to pray was one of the despicable publicans. In the eyes of men the most respected person was, of course, the Pharisee. The man most despised was the publican. But from God's vantage point, the Pharisee who trusted in himself, declaring by the way he lived that he did not need God, was worse than the publican. Every time we live as if we do not need God, it is something despicable and dirty in the eyes of the Lord. This is the reason the Lord Jesus told this story.

Notice what the Pharisee prayed in Luke 18:11-13,

> *The Pharisee stood and prayed thus with himself, God, I thank thee, that I am not as other men are, extortioners, unjust, adulterers, or even as this publican. I fast twice in the week, I give tithes of all that I possess.* [There is no doubt who he is thinking about. Count the number of times he referred to himself.] *And the publican, standing afar off, would not lift up so much as his eyes unto heaven, but smote upon his breast, saying, God be merciful to me a sinner.*

THE REDEMPTION

Notice the redemption in this story. Consider the little word, *"merciful."* What a wonderful word! *"God be merciful to me a sinner."* The word *"merciful"* is a verb form of the same word that is used for mercy seat. The mercy seat, of course, was on the golden lid that covered the ark of the covenant. For the Jews, there was a sacred place where the high priest entered into the Holy of Holies. The Holy of Holies contained what is called the ark of the covenant. It was a box, about a yard in length, made of special wood and covered in gold. The top of the box had a lid made of pure gold. There were angelic beings facing one another; one on one side of the mercy seat, and one on the other side of the lid. There was a space in the center between those two angelic beings. On the Day of Atonement, the high priest would make a sacrifice, take the blood of the innocent animal that was slain, and go into the Holy of Holies, placing the blood on the mercy seat. The place on the top of the ark of the covenant was called the mercy seat.

Every time we live as if we do not need God, it is something despicable and dirty in the eyes of the Lord.

Inside the ark, one could find the Law on tables of stone. The Law cries out that every man is guilty. The Law says that no one can keep the Law perfectly. The Law says everyone is a sinner. The Law says every human being who has ever lived has broken God's Law. The Law cries out that all men deserve to die and go to hell forever. The Law cries out that all of us are guilty. The high priest, on the Day of Atonement, would take the blood of an innocent animal and place the innocent blood on the special golden spot, the mercy seat. The blood covered the Law; the innocent had shed blood for the guilty.

By that means, God made provision for our sins. Someone had to pay. The Old Testament types, in particular as we think of the mercy seat with the innocent animal slain for the guilty, and the blood of the innocent placed on the mercy seat, were beautiful pictures of our Savior. Our innocent, guiltless Savior went to Calvary and shed His blood for our sin. Jesus Christ literally became the mercy seat.

The language the Lord used when He gave this parable would be recognized by His hearers. In particular, the word Christ used for *"merciful"* would be understood as the verb form of the noun used for mercy seat. So, literally, the publican cried out, "God, be the mercy seat for me, a sinner," or "God, the mercy seat for me, a sinner."

The publican was a Jew. Though he hired himself out to the Romans, he knew what the Bible taught. He knew about the innocent blood shed for the guilty; he knew when he walked into the temple that he was a guilty sinner and deserved to be separated from God forever. He knew that his only hope was in the mercy seat. He said, "God, the mercy seat for me, a sinner." The Pharisee prayed to himself, *"I thank thee, that I am not as other men are, extortioners, unjust, adulterers, or even as this publican."* While the Pharisee talked about what he did as if his works justified him before God, the poor publican was crying out, "God, I am a wretched, lost, hell-deserving sinner. God, the mercy seat for me, a sinner." We need to cry out like the publican, "God, the mercy seat for me. It is my only hope. The mercy seat for me, a sinner." This is our only way of redemption, Jesus Christ our mercy seat.

THE RESULT

This story had a surprise ending for the hearers. Remember the despicable, despised publican. The Bible says in Luke 18:14, *"I tell you, this man went down to his house justified."* The publican went in a sinner and came out just as if he were never a sinner. The Pharisee went in a sinner and came out a sinner. *"I tell you, this man went down to his house justified rather than the other: for every one that exalteth himself shall be abased; and he that humbleth himself shall be exalted."* What a result!

When we go to the mercy seat, we come back justified. There is nothing else to justify us. There is no one else that can justify us. There is nothing one can do to be justified. We must only and always say, "God, the mercy seat for me, a sinner."

In Acts 13:39 the Bible says, *"And by him all that believe are justified from all things, from which ye could not be justified by the law of Moses."* We are justified by the Lord Jesus Christ. No matter how

The Parables of Jesus

good one's life is, though it is admirable to try to live a good life, there is nothing to be admired in thinking that one's goodness is better than God. The Bible says that we cannot be justified by the Law of Moses.

Usually, when we read Romans chapter three, we do not get through the entire chapter when using this passage as a proof text or even as a passage for teaching and preaching. Paul talks of the terrible sinfulness of mankind–what an awful list. Romans 3:13-20 says,

> *Their throat is an open sepulchre; with their tongues they have used deceit; the poison of asps is under their lips. Whose mouth is full of cursing and bitterness: their feet are swift to shed blood: destruction and misery are in their ways: and the way of peace have they not known: there is no fear of God before their eyes. Now we know that what things soever the law saith, it saith to them who are under the law: that every mouth may be stopped, and all the world may become guilty before God. Therefore by the deeds of the law there shall no flesh be justified in his sight: for by the law is the knowledge of sin.*

Here we find mankind lost, hell-deserving, hell-bound. Here the whole world is guilty before God. Then we read on in verses twenty-one through twenty-six,

> *But now the righteousness of God without the law is manifested, being witnessed by the law and the prophets; even the righteousness of God which is by faith of Jesus Christ unto all and upon all them that believe: for there is no difference: for all have sinned, and come short of the glory of God; being justified freely by his grace through the redemption that is in Christ Jesus: whom God hath set forth to be a propitiation* [This is the same "mercy seat." The Lord

Jesus is our mercy seat. We could actually say, "Whom God hath set forth to be our mercy seat."] *through faith in his blood, to declare his righteousness for the remission of sins that are past, through the forbearance of God; to declare, I say, at this time his righteousness; that he might be just, and the justifier of him which believeth in Jesus.*

God is good; He is holy; He is righteous; He is always right; He is immutable; He cannot sin; He cannot lie. How can God be good? How can God be holy? How can God be right and let sinners into heaven? How can God be just and do such a thing? Men have done such terrible things. We are all sinners. We are hell-deserving. How can God be good? How can God be holy? How can God be just and let sinners go to heaven and still say He is God?

> *This is our only way of redemption, Jesus Christ our mercy seat.*

The Bible says, *"That he might be just, and the justifier of him which believeth in Jesus."* He is just because He justly demands that sin be paid for. The justice of God demanded that the sin debt must be paid. Because He is a just God, it must be paid.

When our lovely Savior went to Calvary, bled and died for our sin, paid the sin debt in full and tasted death for every man, He satisfied the justice of God. All sin, for all time, for all people, was paid for on Calvary. Now God can be just and be the Justifier. He is just because He demanded that sin be paid for. He is the Justifier because He allows us to come by faith, trusting in the finished work of Christ and asking God to forgive our sin. He puts our record on Calvary where Jesus Christ bled and died for our sin. He puts His record of righteousness and holiness on our record; He imputes His righteousness to our account. So God is just and He is the Justifier.

The Parables of Jesus

When that poor publican came to the temple to pray, he said, "God, the mercy seat for me, a sinner." There is a God in heaven who says, "He left there justified. I am just to justify him because I demanded sin be paid for and it was paid for in the blood of my precious Son." Hallelujah, what a Savior!

In the Garden of Eden, Adam and Eve, our first parents, sinned against God. By the way, I believe the story of Eden, just like God gives it in His Word. He created perfect people and put them in a perfect place. They lived in a dispensation of innocence. They walked in constant fellowship with God. They were clothed in the garment of deity, the Shekinah glory of God. They were innocent; sin had never entered the bloodstream of humanity. God placed them in that beautiful garden. When they sinned, they were separated from God. Physical death came; spiritual death came. They lost their fellowship with the Lord. Their glory was gone. When they were out of that garden and looked back, there was no way to adequately describe what they had lost.

Have you ever lost something? Have you looked back and said, "It is gone"? You felt at the moment it was irretrievably gone. Remember that God came down, walking in the cool of the day. He pronounced judgment on the serpent, the Devil. He also gave the promise of the Redeemer to bruise Satan's head.

What we gain through the finished work of Calvary is more than we ever lost in Eden. To be justified means that God declares that we are just as if we were never sinners–not just as if we had never sinned, but just as if we were never sinners.

People say sometimes, "God has made it so that my sin is forgiven." Yes, He has. But to be justified means that God declares judicially, in the courts of heaven, that we are just as if we were never even sinners. Just as He sees His own dear Son, He sees us through the blood of His Son–just as if we were never sinners.

Think of what we have in the Lord. God has removed our sin as far as the east is from the west. God has buried our sin in the depths of the sea; God has cast our sin behind His back. He has done all of this, but He has done more. We stand before God justified. Friends, that is how we are going to get into heaven. We are going to have entrance freely into heaven because God has declared we are justified.

Think what it meant for Christ to say of that publican, *"He left there justified."* His sins were all gone. God saw him just as if he were never even a sinner. I stand righteous before Him, not on my own merit, but on the merit of His Son who bled and died for me on the cross. I have received His holiness. He took upon Himself my sin. I am justified.

What we gain through the finished work of Calvary is more than we ever lost in Eden.

I heard about a young man that got into trouble with the law. After a little investigating, I asked, "What are they going to do?" Someone said, "They may reduce his sentence or allow him to confess to a lesser charge." Someone else said, "They may let him off with no sentence." Someone else said, "It is possible they could completely erase what happened from the books, and one could go back and check the legal records and not even find that there was ever even an arrest." When I thought about that, I thought, "I have not just had a reduced sentence. I have not simply been found guilty without a sentence. When you check the record in heaven, you do not find any sinful record there!" I have been justified. It is just as if I had never been a sinner. This is what the Lord Jesus has done for me and for all others who have trusted Him as their Savior.

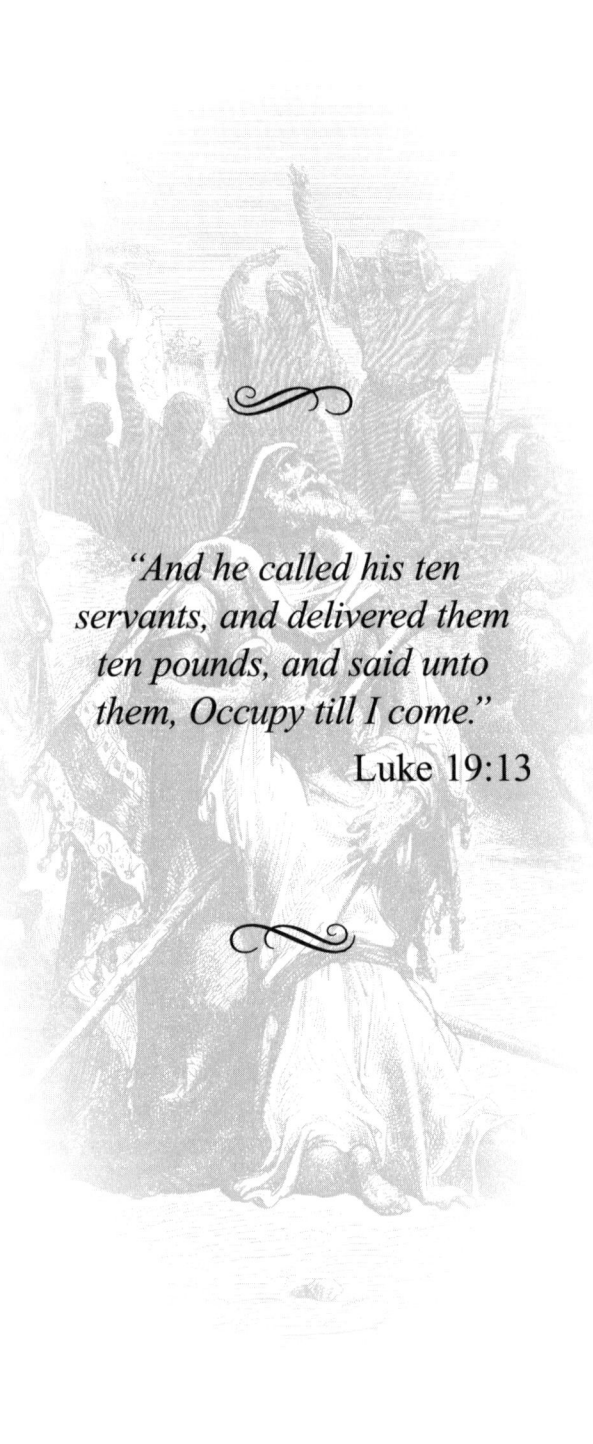

"And he called his ten servants, and delivered them ten pounds, and said unto them, Occupy till I come."

Luke 19:13

Chapter Thirteen

OCCUPY TILL I COME

s the Lord Jesus Christ passed through Jericho, a very curious man desired to see Him. He went out of his way to climb into a tree in order to get a glimpse of Christ. The children's song says, "And as the Savior passed that way, He looked up in the tree, and He said, 'Zacchaeus, you come down, for I am going to your house today.'" In Luke chapter nineteen, we find the dramatic conversion of this publican, Zacchaeus. Immediately following this, the Bible says in Luke 19:11-28,

> *And as they heard these things, he added and spake a parable, because he was nigh to Jerusalem, and because they thought that the kingdom of God should immediately appear. He said therefore, A certain nobleman went into a far country to receive for himself a kingdom, and to return. And he called*

The Parables of Jesus

his ten servants, and delivered them ten pounds, and said unto them, Occupy till I come. But his citizens hated him, and sent a message after him, saying, We will not have this man to reign over us. And it came to pass, that when he was returned, having received the kingdom, then he commanded these servants to be called unto him, to whom he had given the money, that he might know how much every man had gained by trading. Then came the first, saying, Lord, thy pound hath gained ten pounds. And he said unto him, Well, thou good servant: because thou hast been faithful in a very little, have thou authority over ten cities. And the second came, saying, Lord, thy pound hath gained five pounds. And he said likewise to him, Be thou also over five cities. And another came, saying, Lord, behold, here is thy pound, which I have kept laid up in a napkin: for I feared thee, because thou art an austere man: thou takest up that thou layedst not down, and reapest that thou didst not sow. And he saith unto him, Out of thine own mouth will I judge thee, thou wicked servant. Thou knewest that I was an austere man, taking up that I laid not down, and reaping that I did not sow: wherefore then gavest not thou my money into the bank, that at my coming I might have required mine own with usury? And he said unto them that stood by, Take from him the pound, and give it to him that hath ten pounds. (And they said unto him, Lord, he hath ten pounds.) For I say unto you, That unto every one which hath shall be given; and from him that hath not, even that he hath shall be taken away from him. But those mine enemies, which would not that I should reign over them, bring hither, and slay them before me. And when he had thus spoken, he went before, ascending up to Jerusalem.

Note the expression found in the closing part of the thirteenth verse where our Lord Jesus says in this parable, *"Occupy till I come."*

In this passage we find our Lord nearing the end of His earthly ministry. For three and a half years, He has walked with His disciples and He brings this parable in Luke chapter nineteen, saying to them, *"Occupy till I come."*

THE MISUNDERSTANDING OF THE KINGDOM

We must see the misunderstanding of the kingdom. The Bible plainly says in verse eleven, *"And as they heard these things, he added and spake a parable, because he was nigh to Jerusalem, and because they thought that the kingdom of God should immediately appear."* They misunderstood the kingdom. This is quite amazing in light of the fact that they had been with Him for three and a half years. He wanted them to understand His program. He is a King, He has a kingdom, and He does reign; but not yet on this earth. He will reign on this earth for a thousand years, but not yet.

The Bible says, *"And as they heard these things..."* Let us look at the *"things"* they heard. In Luke 19:8 the Bible says, *"And Zacchaeus stood, and said unto the Lord; Behold, Lord, the half of my goods I give to the poor; and if I have taken any thing from any man by false accusation, I restore him fourfold."*

That was one of the things they heard. Notice another thing they heard. Luke 19:9 says, *"And Jesus said unto him, This day is salvation come to this house, forsomuch as he also is a son of Abraham."*

In verse ten the Bible says, *"For the Son of man is come to seek and to save that which was lost."* That was another thing they heard. No doubt when they heard this talk about Abraham and they heard about gaining back that which was lost, they thought about the kingdom. They were nigh to Jerusalem at the time of the Passover.

The Parables of Jesus

The historian Josephus tells us that as many as two million people made their way to the city of Jerusalem during the Passover feast. So as they neared Jerusalem, they found people camped everywhere. This was the prime moment for Jesus Christ to make the grand announcement that He was going to set up His kingdom, overthrow the Roman government, and finally, the Jews would reign with their King. In the hearts of these disciples, they had a mistaken idea. He was not talking about gaining for them the kingdom they had lost. He was talking about bringing lost souls to Himself.

The Bible says in Luke 19:11, *"And as they heard these things, he added and spake a parable, because he was nigh to Jerusalem, and because they thought that the kingdom of God should immediately appear."*

There are many people who are mistaken about His kingdom. Christ came to this earth and lived a sinless life. He offered Himself as king and was rejected. The Bible says, *"He came unto his own, and his own received him not"* (John 1:11). He went to the cross and bore the sin debt of the whole world. He bled and died, tasting death for every man. He was buried in a borrowed tomb, and He came forth from the grave alive forevermore.

The Bible says in Philippians 2:9-11,

> *Wherefore God also hath highly exalted him, and given him a name which is above every name: that at the name of Jesus every knee should bow, of things in heaven, and things in earth, and things under the earth; and that every tongue should confess that Jesus Christ is Lord, to the glory of God the Father.*

Jesus Christ certainly is a King, but He does not yet rule and reign on this earth. If that is not His program in the here and now, what is His program? At this time, His program is for His servants to do His work and to go into all the world and preach the gospel to every creature.

At this point, it seems very fitting for this parable to bring the whole matter of following and serving Christ to a conclusion. There are people trying to build a kingdom from the earth. They are trying in some way to improve society, improve life, to bring God up to people from the earth. They want to sort of "work it up" from among men. But Christ's kingdom will not come that way. It will not be worked up from among men.

The church of the living God has been and will always be a minority of holy people living in an unholy world. If you have the idea that everyone is going to become a believer, that the whole world is going to come to Christ, you have a mistaken idea about God's work. I know at times it seems to be a very troublesome thing to think how few know the Lord compared to how many have lived and died and how many are alive today. I must be reminded that the way to heaven is one way, not many ways. Jesus Christ said, *"I am the way, the truth, and the life: no man cometh unto the Father, but by me"* (John 14:6).

We can wish for a better world, but our better world is the world that is to come; it is not this world. I want to be as responsible a citizen as I possibly can be, living in a way that does not bring reproach upon the name of Christ. I want to live an exemplary Christian life, but I do not want to get caught up in the idea that we are going to work up the kingdom from down here. It is just not going to happen. So many are giving so much effort to making the world a better place from which to go to hell.

THE MEANING OF THIS PARABLE

What does this parable mean? Some people think this is the same parabolic teaching as the teaching given in the parable of the talent. But there is quite a difference to be found.

The Parables of Jesus

In the parable of the talents, each received a different number of talents. In the parable of the pounds, all of the servants received the same. It is an entirely different parable. The Bible says, *"He said therefore, A certain nobleman went into a far country to receive for himself a kingdom, and to return."*

Our Lord, who shed His precious blood, had that precious blood presented before God the Father. The sacrifice of the Savior was accepted before God. The payment was made in the precious blood of Christ. Receipt was given in the glorious resurrection of our Savior.

When Pilate asked Him if He were a king, Christ said to him in John 18:37, *"For this cause came I into the world."* In this parable the Lord Jesus said that He went into a far country to receive a kingdom and to return. When He went, He called His ten servants and delivered them ten pounds and said to them, *"Occupy till I come."* That is what God has given us to do–to occupy till He comes.

We are His servants, and He has given us a pound. There is no doubt that this pound represents our responsibility to do His work, to witness for our Savior, to tell people about Jesus Christ. Every Christian has this responsibility. No child of God is exempt from this responsibility. Our King came from heaven and bled and died on the cross. He has gone back to glory to receive a kingdom. He is coming again.

Notice what the Bible says, *"But his citizens hated him, and sent a message after him, saying, We will not have this man to reign over us."* This sounds like Psalm 2, does it not? *"The heathen rage, and the people imagine a vain thing."* They do not want anyone to reign over them.

The citizens sent a message to the king, "We hate the king. We do not want the king to reign over us." We are left on the earth as His servants with a pound among a citizenry that hates the King, among people who do not want the King to reign over them. Here

we find ourselves in a world that is against God, a world that is against our Christ.

What are we to do? We are to occupy till He comes; we are to let God use us for His glory. We are to get as many citizens as possible to turn from their antagonism toward the King, to love Him and have affection for the King.

You may ask, "Can it be done?" Every believer is a living testimony that it can be done. It has been done. There was a time when I was in darkness and a time when I did not want Christ. There was a time that I did not want Him to rule over me. There was a time in the darkness of sin and rebellion I did not want God. But someone used his pound; he came to me and brought me from being an antagonistic citizen to an affectionate follower of Jesus Christ. This is the meaning of this parable.

So many are giving so much effort to making the world a better place from which to go to hell.

THE MEETING WITH THE KING

The King is returning. When He comes again, He will come to an unbelieving, Christ-rejecting world; but that is not the message of this passage. We find these servants meeting their king.

In all of our preaching on the wickedness of our world and the punishment and judgment of the unsaved, we somehow forget that we are going to meet our King. We will be examined to see what we have done with what He left us.

Consider II Corinthians 5:10, *"For we must all appear before the judgment seat of Christ; that every one may receive the things done in his body, according to that he hath done, whether it be good or bad."* The judgment seat of Christ is for Christians. It is not a judgment of our salvation; it is a judgment of our works, of what "sort" they are. The moment we trust Christ as Savior, we have everlasting life. Instantaneously, we are born from above into God's family. When that takes place, we change judgments. We were headed toward the Great White Throne judgment where every lost person will meet God and be cast into a lake of fire. However, at the moment we trust Christ as Savior, we are destined for the judgment seat of Christ.

The judgment seat is for the believer. The believer's judge is the Lord Jesus Christ. Their judgment takes place immediately after the Rapture, or the catching away of the church. Consider again II Corinthians 5:10. The Bible says, *"For we must all appear before the judgment seat of Christ; that every one may receive the things done in his body, according to that he hath done, whether it be good or bad."*

In this context of Scripture, examine the eleventh verse, *"Knowing therefore the terror of the Lord, we persuade men; but we are made manifest unto God; and I trust also are made manifest in your consciences."* This verse is not about unsaved people feeling the terror of the Lord. Verse eleven speaks about the heart of a believer as he thinks of that moment when he answers personally to the King for the life he has lived as a Christian.

All of us who are believers will look into the face of Jesus Christ and answer for the way we have lived our Christian lives. There are times when this is the only thing that gets me through. When I am misunderstood or falsely accused, when someone is absolutely convinced that something is right when it is all wrong, I think, "Lord, there is coming a day when the truth will be revealed; it will all come out."

There are times that this same thought of the judgment causes me to tremble. I tremble to think that any excuse I might use for not using my pound, my opportunity to witness, will not stand up when I meet Christ at the judgment seat.

Occupy Till I Come

Look at the parable again. Here the king has come back. The citizens hated him in verse fourteen. In verse twenty-seven the Bible says, *"But those mine enemies, which would not that I should reign over them, bring hither, and slay them before me."* These are the unsaved who remained unsaved. Those citizens were filled with hatred before the king.

Look at his followers for a moment. In verse fifteen the Bible says,

> *And it came to pass, that when he was returned, having received the kingdom, then he commanded these servants to be called unto him, to whom he had given the money, that he might know how much every man had gained by trading.*

Remember, this pound represents our witnessing; our doing the King's business. Occupying until He comes means doing His work. His work is the work of telling others about Him and bringing the lost to Christ.

> *All of us who are believers will look into the face of Jesus Christ and answer for the way we have lived our Christian lives.*

> *Then came the first, saying, Lord, thy pound hath gained ten pounds. And he said unto him, Well, thou good servant: because thou hast been faithful in a very little, have thou authority over ten cities. And the second came, saying, Lord, thy pound hath gained five pounds. And he said likewise to him, Be thou also over five cities. And another came, saying, Lord, behold, here is thy pound, which I have kept laid up in a napkin.*

In other words, he said, "I did nothing with it. I did not witness to anyone. I did not try to get any of these citizens who hated you to become your followers. I did not try to speak to any of these citizens who hated you, who are part of this lost, unregenerate world. I did not try to get any of them to know You and love You. But, oh, Lord, I know You and love You." There is not much evidence that we love Him when we do not tell others about Him.

He said, "I hid it in a napkin." I have circled that word napkin in my Bible and written it out again in bold letters, NAPKIN, and put an exclamation mark. What are my napkins? "I did not use it because I got so busy doing other things. I have a lot of office work to do, a lot of administrative work to do. I have other important things to do." Many of us in God's work have hidden the responsibility to witness in many napkins. We have hidden it in the office. We have hidden it in the school. We have hidden it in so many secondary things, things that were important, but not most important. We are very busy, but no one is exempt from occupying till He comes, doing His work to try to win the lost.

Occupying until He comes means doing His work. His work is the work of telling others about Him and bringing the lost to Christ.

What about these citizens that hate Him? The Bible says, *"But his citizens hated him."* What have we done with our pound to change their attitude about Christ; to bring them to know the Lord as Savior? The servant said, "I did not do anything with my pound. I hid it in a napkin." What is your napkin?

Many say, "I have worked hard. I have been busy with lots of activities. But as far as telling people about Christ, as far as making an impact on the citizens that hate Him, I hid all of that in a napkin." Christ is not pleased with that.

Your programs and activities are important. But if you have made a napkin out of them, just a place to hide your responsibility to

Occupy Till I Come

witness, it will not work when you meet the Lord. When will the King return? It is not a matter of whether, but of when He will return. I feel a terror in my heart because others are going to hell. I have hidden my pound in a napkin, and I could have made a difference.

We can make a good case for letting many things become our napkin, but it will not stand up when we meet the Lord. May the thought of His coming serve as a wake-up call to us. Christ said, *"Occupy till I come."*

Sunday School materials are available for use in conjunction with *The Parables of Jesus*.
For a complete listing of available materials from Crown Publications, please call 1-877 AT CROWN or write to: P.O. Box 159 ❖ Powell, TN ❖ 37849

Visit us on the Web at
www.FaithfortheFamily.com
"*A Website for the Christian Family*"

ABOUT THE AUTHOR

Clarence Sexton is the pastor of the Temple Baptist Church and founder of Crown College in Knoxville, Tennessee. He has written more than twenty books and booklets. He speaks in conferences throughout the United States and has conducted training sessions for pastors and Christian workers in several countries around the world. He and his wife, Evelyn, have been married for thirty-six years. They have two grown sons and six grandchildren. For more information about the ministry of Clarence Sexton, visit our website at www.FaithfortheFamily.com.

OTHER HELPFUL BOOKS BY CLARENCE SEXTON:

THE LORD IS MY SHEPHERD

EARNESTLY CONTEND FOR THE FAITH

THE CHRISTIAN HOME

TRUTHS EVERY CHRISTIAN NEEDS TO KNOW

LORD, SEND A REVIVAL

THE PARABLES OF JESUS VOLUME 1

ISSUES OF LIFE ANSWERED FROM THE BIBLE

THE CONCLUSION OF THE WHOLE MATTER VOLUME 1